ORO
EDITIONS

URBAN LESSONS OF THE VENETIAN SQUARES

Kenneth M. Moffett, AIA

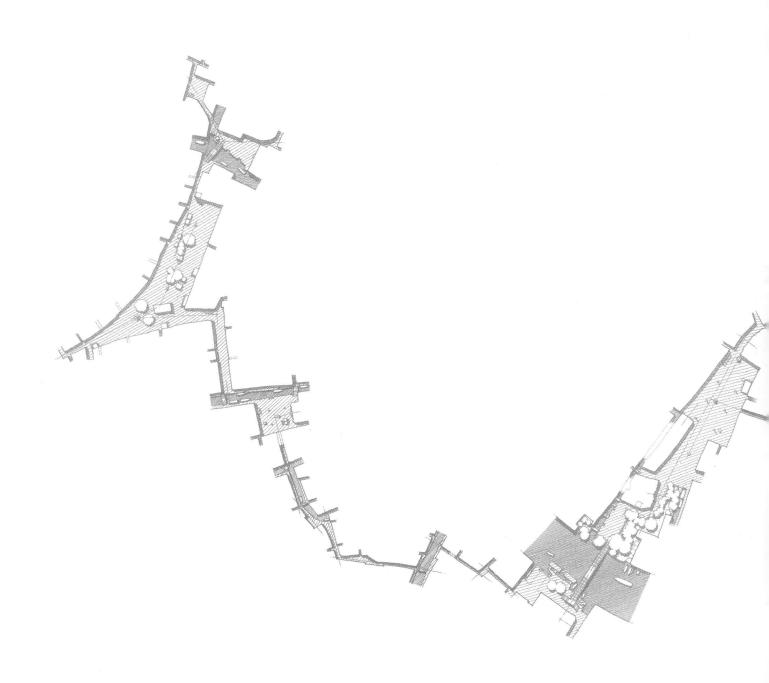

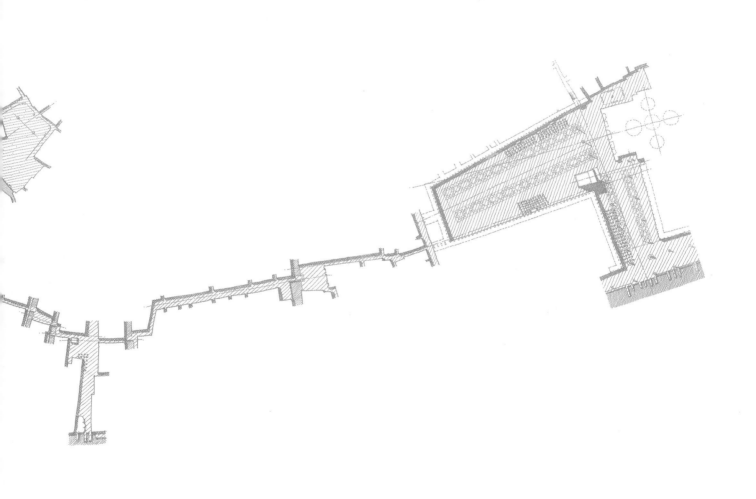

Publishers of Architecture, Art, and Design
Gordon Goff: Publisher

www.oroeditions.com
info@oroeditions.com

Published by ORO Editions

Graphic Design: Ahankara Art
ORO Project Coordinator: Kirby Anderson
Illustrations, diagrams, and photos are by the author except where noted.

10 9 8 7 6 5 4 3 2 1 First Edition

Library of Congress data available upon request.
World Rights: Available

ISBN: 978-1-954081-63-5

Color Separations and Printing: ORO Group Ltd.
Printed in China.

International Distribution: www.oroeditions.com/distribution

ORO Editions makes a continuous effort to minimize the overall carbon footprint of its publications. As part of this goal, ORO Editions, in association with Global ReLeaf, arranges to plant trees to replace those used in the manufacturing of the paper produced for its books. Global ReLeaf is an international campaign run by American Forests, one of the world's oldest nonprofit conservation organizations. Global ReLeaf is American Forests' education and action program that helps individuals, organizations, agencies, and corporations improve the local and global environment by planting and caring for trees.

Also by Kenneth M. Moffett:
• *Forming and Centering: Foundational Aspects of Architectural Design*
• *Architecture's New Strangeness: A 21st Century Cult of Peculiarity*

For Cindy

"Venice is a maze of alleys, secluded courtyards, bridges, archways, tortuous passages, dead ends, quaysides, dark overhung back streets and sudden sunlit squares."

– Jan Morris

Table of Contents

Preface

Among the urban places visited on my first trip to Europe in 1968, Venice made far and away the most influential impression. A fascination with this most unusual of Western cities has remained through the years and the visits since, despite its ongoing fate as a themed attraction for international tourists. This narrative makes an effort to identify the aspects of the Venetian squares that exemplify an admirable urbanism, the test of time arguably rendering them as instructive today as they were in past centuries. A survey of urban spaces in modern America then tells us how those findings are manifest today, and about aspects of the findings from the "campi" that still need better attention.

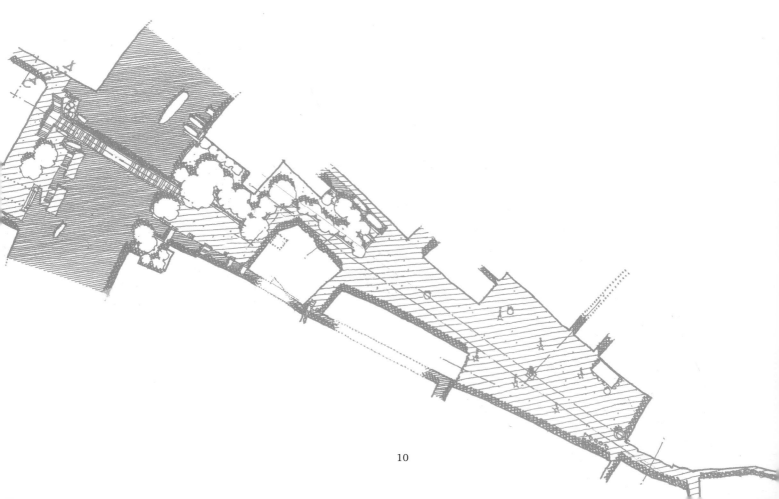

Introduction

Modern-day developments in urban design include a significant rediscovery of some urban values that predate the advent of modernism in architecture and planning, sometimes under the rubric of "new urbanism." Advocacy for better definition of neighborhoods and town centers, a reduced preponderance of street-side parking lots, and an improved respect for the pedestrian experience are among the movement's hallmarks. In addition to a renewed appreciation of the merits of inner suburbs of the early 20th century, as in the work of DPZ, Moule & Polyzoides, and others, this rediscovery has extended to precedents from the old world, as in the new town designs of Léon Krier and Demetri Porphyrios.

However, it's fair to say that on the evidence of new world planning and development, much of this thinking seems to call for the weaving of car parking through the recast urban fabric, to afford the dual illusions of accessibility and viability.[1] We have lived within and alongside cars and their thoroughfares for so long that it seems we can feel lost without them, and a square featuring no parked or bypassing traffic can evidently be sometimes thought to feel a bit empty and forlorn, a fact which is an understandable if ultimately sad testimony about some American urban perceptions.

As a test case of sorts to help inform the successes and failings of modern urban open space, a useful strategy would be to somehow remove the cars and streets from the equation: not as a realistic goal for urbanism today, but as a lens through which to identify a family of attributes that could realistically contribute to successful urban places. The only city in the Western world where this condition actually prevails in reality is Venice, Italy. Alone among the Old World's cities and towns that are the USA's urban patrimony, Venice has the unique distinction of being a truly pedestrian urban environment.[2] With this in mind, it seems reasonable to see if Venice could call across the centuries with some insights for modern-day urbanism.

1 Venice and the Campi

Just as narrow, labyrinthine walkways define Venice's connective pedestrian experience, its comparable system of canals has no true equal, and the city's panoply of architectural monuments and works of art is, in relation to its size, the equal of any in the world. But another pervasive defining system, which has received less attention from scholars and tourists alike, may have more to offer in terms of lessons for the cause of humane urbanism today. This would be the array of squares scattered throughout the city, serving variously as civic spaces, circulation junctions, forecourts for churches, and centers for neighborhood life. In terms of the urban experience, they provide points of orientation and destination in the pedestrian labyrinth, giving the sometimes chaotic Venetian urban tour a sense of sequence, order, and objective.

While Piazza San Marco takes its place as by far the largest and best known of the Venetian squares, it is an anomaly in several respects, and the only urban space in Venice to be called a piazza. Each of the others is called a campo, which means "field," a designation for urban squares which is unique to Venice. Originally the campi were indeed half-rural spaces where animals grazed and food was grown.[3,4] Their fascinating and important histories aside, the primary purpose here is to observe what a pertinent selection of these squares may have to tell us in terms of some useful and perhaps surprising lessons for urbanism in this day and age.[5] Observations on each of these selected campi follow, supplemented with a variety of diagrams and illustrations. Interspersed among these and following after are a number of "sidebars" on subjects that are pertinent to all the campi and to this urban experience as a whole. Next comes a set of "findings" that bring together the varied mix of observations into specific recommendations, based on the collective lessons the Venetian squares offer for vibrant urban spaces, when freed from the demands of the automobile. And following that, the findings are brought forth to seek some applications to the urban square in the USA of modern times.

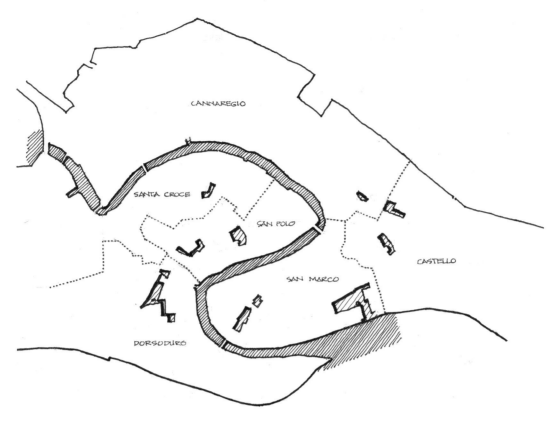

1.1 The Sestieri of Venice, with footprints of the selected Campi.

Sidebar: Geography

A consequence of Venice's lagoon setting is its flatness. While some towns and cities in the Old and New Worlds—Siena, Prague, San Francisco—feature dramatic topography among their defining characteristics and are notably appealing for this reason, it's fair to say that the lack of this "variable" affords yet another reason that Venice should prove eminently useful as a laboratory for observing exterior settings of urban life. Lacking prospects, belvederes, slopes, monumental steps—elements of urban vocabulary that are intrinsically dependent on the vagaries of the topography of place—the interactions of other more readily composed and modifiable elements can be more clearly observed.

The aggregated island flatlands of Venice, of which there are more than a hundred, are apportioned into six administrative sectors—sestieri—which subdivide the two shaking hands of the city with some degree of geographic logic (Fig. 1.1). To the west and south of the great *S* of the Grand Canal, the sestiere of *San Croce* comes first upon arrival by car, extending west into its necessarily compromised industrial, maritime, and car park extremities. *San Polo* occupies a central zone which includes the crowded routes leading to the Rialto Bridge. Over the Rialto, the sestiere of *San Marco*, incorporating the eponymous Piazza, is wrapped by the lower reaches of the Grand

Canal. *Dorsoduro*, named for the relative solidity of its mudflat underpinnings, lies to the south, overlooking the Giudecca Canal, and the islands of Giudecca which flank this wide waterway to the south are considered part of Dorsoduro. To the north, the quieter and more attenuated morphology of *Cannaregio* stretches across the top, terminated at the west by the train station. Lastly, *Castello,* named for a fort built by the first Venetian settlers, extends into the more remote and less touristed neighborhoods to the east. Each of these sestieri is anchored by one or more of the campi to be "visited" on this tour of observation.

S. Giacomo chapel, Vera

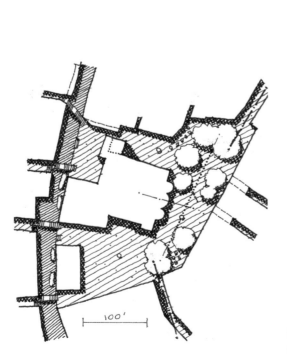

1.2 Ground Plan: Campo San Giacomo dell'Orio. All plans are oriented with north to top.

Sestiere San Croce: Campo San Giacomo dell'Orio

There is no deliberate ordering of this set of squares and observations about them, aside from the fact that each in turn is relatively close to the next. Though this first square is just three hundred yards

1.3 Campo San Giacomo: Apsidal view of Chiesa di San Giacomo dell'Orio.
The origin of the name of the campo and the church is obscure. The church's west exposure and entry face the little Campiello dei Piovan.

from the railroad station, Campo San Giacomo dell'Orio seems a world apart, like a neighborhood center that could be the hub of a modest village (Fig. 1.2).[6] In a real sense it is, though it has been compromised to some degree by the expansion of Venice's rampant tourism into the city's peripheries. A parish church turns its back to proffer a muscular series of apsidal chapels, its entry exposure facing an adjoining campiello. Arrival from that direction involves some effective misdirection: the campiello gives no hint of the unexpected payoff, reached through a narrow gap beside the church tower, of the larger and more complex space beyond (Figs. 1.3, 1.4). In contrast, routes arriving from the north and south focus directly into this campo, but its true nature is again concealed, due to the

1.4 Campo San Giacomo: Looking west upon entry toward Campiello dei Morti.
This space is contiguous with Campo San Giacomo. The church tower anchors the ensemble and defines a narrow passage which is the route from the Campiello dei Piovan beyond, fronting the Rio San Giacomo. A campiello is a small campo, of which there are many in Venice: a sidebar narrative will discuss their typology.

framing effect of the narrow street walls, the screening aspect of trees, and the complexity of the space's footprint. This framing of an incomplete and intriguing excerpt affords a pleasurable sense of anticipation (Fig. 1.5).

The campo itself is engagingly ambiguous, being partially separated into sub-spaces by the interposition of the church's footprint. This spatial dynamic encourages a desirable variety in the activity level of these zones, ranging from being rather open and empty at the south, through a central zone of pedestrians, bench sitters, and children's ballgames, to the more populous cafés and umbrella tables at the north. This north-south sequence is formalized by a subtle alignment of wellheads and flagpoles along an axis of paving stones, implying a linear axis for the square, while the square's boundaries tell a contrasting story of spatial rotation. Another subtly ironic contrast exists between the church's rotational centerpiece and the square's nearly monolithic sidewalls, for the space theatrically showcases the church's assertive but inactive apses and flanks, while the campo's flattened perimeter is highly varied in color, fenestration, skyline, and activity (Figs. 1.6, 1.7).

1.5 Campo San Giacomo: View south to entry.
The compressed and shady approach focuses on the contrasting sunny and leafy space beyond, while concealing much of the campo's nature until the end of the approach is reached. No route to this campo, whether from the railroad station or from others of the campi that follow, is very direct; as a result, it exists in a pleasurable sense of isolation.

1.6 Campo San Giacomo: Its space revealed upon entry. The campo's rotational space contrasts with its axial entryways, and the colorful concave sidewall contrasts with the bulging apses of the Chiesa San Giacomo opposite. The U shape of the campo results in a constant reveal of evolving spatial conditions.

1.7 Campo San Giacomo: Sketch looking west to north.
The wide-angle format showcases the effect—defined by the central church volume—of the campo's horseshoe footprint, which leads to blind corners and hints of the canal beyond.

Sestiere San Polo: Campo San Polo

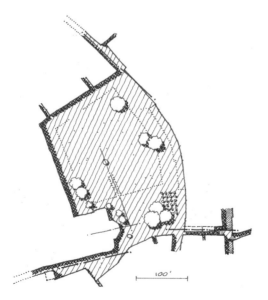

1.8 Ground Plan: Campo San Polo.
Note the three different entrance types at three corners.

Campo San Polo, Venice's largest, also stands curiously alone, which enhances the surprise upon entry (Fig. 1.8). This aspect of surprise, which recurs in various guises throughout Venice, is also fostered by the particular and varied morphology of the campo's three principal entries from the street network, each exemplifying a different type of obscured-entry approach. From the north via the small foyer-like space of Rio Terà Sant'Antonio, indirection and deflection are the key, with the Campo

1.9 Campo San Polo: View to south upon entry from north.
The concave east face sweeps in toward the "tableau" of elements and activity at the south. The open, austere character of much of the campo is evident in this view from the 1970s.

sidewall beyond bending and faceting around to completely delay revelation of the space until the last corner is turned (Fig. 1.9). Once within the space, aspects of its shape and pavement imply a rough cross-axial symmetry, but one bearing no relationship to its entries, which slip in inconspicuously at various corners. Even more circumspect than the north entry, a small triangular sub-space enters the Campo at its southwest corner through an angled pinch-point, the campo again fully concealed until the last moment. Even then, a rotation around the adjacent church's apse is required for the entire space to be revealed.

Lastly, a different and unusual screening effect is accomplished to the southeast by the intervention of a complex, Piranesian covered loggia passage, involving flights of steps and unexpected spatial shifts. The passage obscures views of the approaching campo until the façade

of the space is penetrated, affording an instantaneous spatial expansion. This version of approach, which recurs in several guises among the campi, is the most dramatic among the several means: not only is the entryway passage focused and narrow, but it's enclosed overhead, and dim, contrasting in every respect with the space beyond.

In the past, Campo San Polo accommodated bullfights, mass sermons, and masked balls, while nowadays it is sometimes the scene of open-air markets, as well as a popular venue for open-air concerts, screenings, and Carnival activities. Its largely empty west half certainly facilitates these occasional mass-attendance uses, but under everyday circumstances the square is far from *seeming* empty, saying something about how to make an urban space just interesting enough without overreaching into an excess of busyness. Its south

19

1.10 Campo San Polo: View to west upon entry from north.
More recent views reveal some brighter and more varied colors on these once uniformly neutral façades. As simple an element as paint can and does have a significant effect on the impact of these spaces. That said, this stretch of understated uniformity, while displaying a variegated pattern of fenestration, seems more fitting to this campo's character.

side collects a tableau of activating and interacting anchors, including cafés, kiosks, a monumental flagpole, trees, and a church's projecting apse. That modest element serves a more conventionally resolved urban role here than at Campo San Giacomo, framing as it does the south end with its players and almost defining a stage, with the flanking "backstage" entries noted above, to which the long concave east sidewall returns like the flank of a theater.

A largely consistent eave height, as well as extensive continuities of sidewall color, further contribute to this cohesive and focused spatial quality (Fig. 1.10). A wellhead marking the physical center of the campo works in combination with its roughly equilateral dimensions and relative uniformity in other respects to evoke a sense of rather unfocused calm. Completely paved as well, given these characteristics the square could easily seem arid and empty when its traditional special events are not in action, and indeed did so on the occasion of the author's first visit, despite its interesting ensemble to the south. In more recent times, though, it has been somewhat redeemed by the color, massing, texture, and shade of several groves of modest trees which have matured in the interval. Tellingly, the ephemeral realities of plant material have afforded, in a way, a more important component of this square's success than have the merits of its centuries-old architecture.

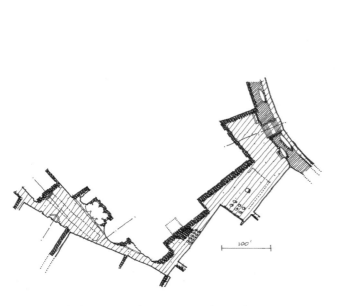

1.11 Ground Plan: Campi dei Frari (to right) and San Rocco (to left).
Due to the elbow of narrow connecting ways, these two campi are completely isolated from each other. In contrast, the spaces that follow, which center on Campo Santa Margherita, make up an unusually extensive connected spatial sequence.

1.12 Campo dei Frari: Sketch looking southwest.
The echelon of three receding gables, each with its roundel window, draws the eye to the pinch point at the back corner. The church tower has a pronounced lean, as do many in Venice.

Sestiere San Polo: Campi dei Frari & San Rocco

As with Campo San Polo, Campo dei Frari is isolated from relatively nearby campi by a labyrinth of extremely narrow passages. The footprint of Campo dei Frari ("Campo of the Friars") bears some superficial resemblances to that of San Giacomo in that the square wraps two faces of a church (Fig. 1.11). But in this case the Franciscan church of Santa Maria Gloriosa dei Frari is the largest Italian Gothic edifice in Venice, and it completely dominates the open space. Café and shop activity are minimal, as are trees and other freestanding features; the only relief from the massive masonry walls and pavements is the contiguous canal quay to the east, but this is insufficient to relieve the severe aspect of the space.

As if to make the most of this opportunity, the footprint and façades of the church work with the campo to form a compelling exercise in recursion. Three gabled masonry façades, each marked by a roundel window, step back in space while becoming smaller in scale: the main façade leads to a side chapel, leading in turn to a smaller apsidal chapel in the shadowy space beyond the campo (Fig. 1.12). A narrow gap beckons as a relief from the bareness of the space, leading to a subsidiary miniature of the arrowhead shape of the campo itself. Here, a sidewalk café is in scale with its surroundings and activates them, while a comparable small array of umbrella tables in the campo itself seems dwarfed and hardly noticed.

At the end of this space, the apsidal chapel's projecting volume defines a pinch point which leads to the narrow passage of Salizada San Rocco, alongside the church's assertive row of apsidal chapel façades. The semicircular apse itself protrudes to create yet another pinch point, leading in turn to another compressed triangle of space, which is Campo San Rocco. Even though defined by the same church edifice as Campo dei Frari, there is no sense of continuity or relationship between these two spaces. The square is named for both the Chiesa di San Rocco and the Scuola Grande di San Rocco, the latter well-known for its collection of paintings by Tintoretto. Defined by these imposing monuments of Venetian Renaissance architecture, the square is intimidated by their tall, assertive presences: if the Campo dei Frari is dominated by its architecture, Campo San Rocco seems claustrophobic. In contrast to expansive San Polo, which achieves a balance of activity and quietude, San Rocco is compressed and overwhelmed, both in terms simply of spatial proportion and with regard to its massive façades, each trying to shout down the other. Even a "runner" of pavement pattern leading to the church façade is bent out of shape by converging sidewalls.

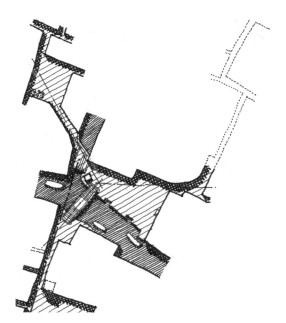

1.13 Ground Plan: Campo San Pantalon and Campiello Mosca.
Campiello Mosca ("Fly") is at the upper left, the path from Campo dei Frari at the upper right, and the path to Campo Santa Margherita is below.

Sestiere Dorsoduro: Campi San Pantalon, Santa Margherita, & San Barnaba

Another connection of narrow calles leads to Campo San Pantalon (Fig. 1.13). This space initiates one of the most exhilarating spatial sequences in Venice.

1.14 Campo San
Pantalon: View to
south.
The bridge beyond
the kiosk leads to the
contrasting small space
of Calle de la Chiesa.
This necks down to a
narrow slot that leads
in turn to Campo Santa
Margherita.

Like Campo dei Frari, the square is both the forecourt for a church and the quayside for a canal, but here the experiential equation is completely different. The pedestrian route swings unexpectedly into this triangular space through one of its corners, alongside the great rough slab of the unfinished church façade, to confront an axial vista of one of Venice's busiest canals, always full of waterborne traffic. Two dramatic bridges converge at the apex of the space in a busy node of pedestrian circulation, a souvenir kiosk serving as a focal point for this nexus of spatial and circulatory forces (Fig. 1.14). Though large enough to accommodate shops or cafés, Campo San Pantalon offers little such activity, and has more the quality of a busy thoroughfare, dominated by its aggressive surroundings and traffic.

One of its bridges leads to a diagonal byway to the northwest and makes another corner entry into the little Campiello Mosca. A simple square in plan, the space is remarkably enlivened by a diagonal axis defined by points of entry at opposed corners: rectangular volumes become serried echelons, and the space seems divided into rakish triangles. Yet despite the busy popularity of this route, the space has the quality of a peaceful refuge harboring quiet cafés, a calm prologue for what follows.

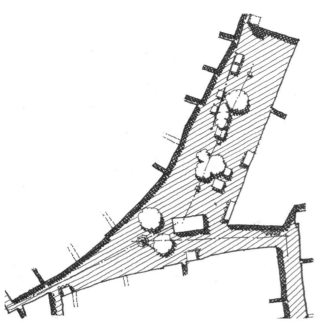

1.15 Ground Plan: Campo Santa Margherita. The path from Calle de la Chiesa and Campo San Pantalon is at the top. The former Scuola dei Varotari defines a dogleg into Rio Terà Canal at the lower right.

At San Pantalon, an impressive bridge crosses the bustling Rio Novo canal to the tiny forecourt space of the Calle de la Chiesa, which necks down into a tall, rather daunting passage. As at Campo San Giacomo, the approach looks directly into a framed view of a larger open space, but one which is again ambiguous in its nature and extent, with glimpses of trees beyond trees and market sheds arrayed one beyond the next. This is Campo Santa Margherita, typified by aspects shared with no other Venetian square (Fig. 1.15). A preeminent market campo, it bustles with vendors and their kiosks and umbrellas in the morning, while by afternoon the character of the space changes completely with the dismantling and removal of the market kiosks, becoming calm and austere. Its sidewalls are characteristically continuous with only the narrowest of gaps. Sottoportegi and alleyways line up along the sweep of the extended western flank, leading to a parallel canal where deliveries are made from boats directly to their endpoints in the sheer flank of urban fabric.[7] The campo boundaries incorporate greengrocers, cafés, wine shops, tobacconists, and residences, plus the tower of the former Church of Santa

1.16 Campo Santa
Margherita: View north
toward Campo San
Pantalon.
The trees in the middle
of the space, as opposed
to adjoining a sidewall,
are unusual among
the campi, as are the
intervening market
stalls. As a result
the campo is usually
perceived in a series of
vignettes rather than
overall views.

Margherita, repurposed successively as a
cinema and a local arts center. When the
trees are in leaf and the market is underway,
the campo's shape and extent remain hard
to perceive, no matter where one stands
within its main space (Fig. 1.16). Abetting
this ambiguity, the spatial footprint begins
as a rectangle but gradually morphs into
a funnel-like shape, the convex sidewall
pressing inward, inducing movement and
mystery by constantly obscuring a full
view of what lies ahead.

The unusual feature of a freestanding
building, originally housing the Scuola
dei Varotari (tanner and fur vendors),
anchors the south end to add a further

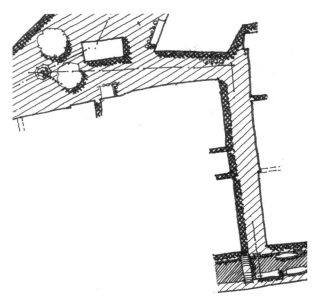

1.17 Ground Plan: Rio Terà Canal.
Despite Venice's image as a city of narrow, winding streets, many have long, straight stretches, but few are as wide as this street became once its canal was filled in. The long offsets at each end completely isolate the street from the two adjoining campi, rendering each a surprising find on approach.

measure of spatial sleight of hand. From the north, this building is obscured by the intervening trees, and blends with the walls of the campo, but from other entries the simple fact of its placement crafts two completely different spatial experiences:

- From the southwest vertex, this building sits center stage and casts the campo proper into the background to the left, while defining a tributary passage to the right.
- From the east, this passage *is* the experience, with the campo quite obscured, only to be revealed once the acute-angled corner is passed.

This demonstrates a third entry strategy: neither axially focused nor deflected, entry is off to the side of the bypassing route, in a parallel rather than terminating relationship (Fig. 1.17).

Exiting via this route leads abruptly to another right-angle turn, revealing Rio Terà Canal, a comparatively broad and straight street-like space. Like a number of wider walkways in Venice, the aptly named route once comprised a canal with a narrower path alongside. (Several campi also once featured canals, Santa Margherita and San Polo among them.) In one of the felicitous tableaus among many in Venice, a fruit and vegetable vendor has anchored his boat in the canal at the south end of this space, its sweeping shade canopy contributing to the theatrical, stage-like quality of the ensemble (Fig. 1.18). Precursor barges are said to have occupied this desirable position for centuries.

1.18 Rio Terà Canal:
View to south.
The street leads
from Campo Santa
Margherita to Campo
San Barnaba, across
the Rio di San Barnaba
and to the left. Facing
almost due south, the
shaded street showcases
a sunlit tableau.

Crossing the bridge alongside the vendor's barge, one turns east to complete a zigzag link between Santa Margherita and Campo San Barnaba (Fig. 1.19). Perhaps the closest to a perfect square of all the "squares" in Venice, it is a modest space similar in area to San Pantalon but much less frenetically activated, having instead an urbane dignity befitting its proportions. Its varied perimeters, featuring an imposing church, the canal with its boats and bridges, lively cafés and shops, and a widely varied array of wall openings and colors, help make the square one of the most ingratiating in Venice (Fig. 1.20).[8] Enlivened by pedestrian

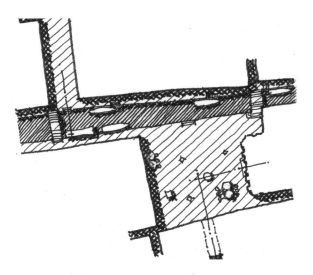

1.19 Ground Plan: Campo San Barnaba.

27

1.20a View of Campo San Barnaba, south to north.

1.20b View of the Campo from the sottoportego leading south.

traffic drawing diagonals across the foursquare pavement, it nonetheless seems a true place of destination with a sense of neighborly repose.

    Two final figures give a sense of the preceding overall spatial sequence, showing the progression centering on Campo Santa Margherita in plan and in a series of sequential eye-level views (Figs. 1.21, 1.22).

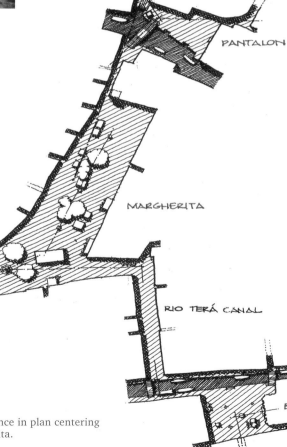

1.21 The combined sequence in plan centering on Campo Santa Margherita.

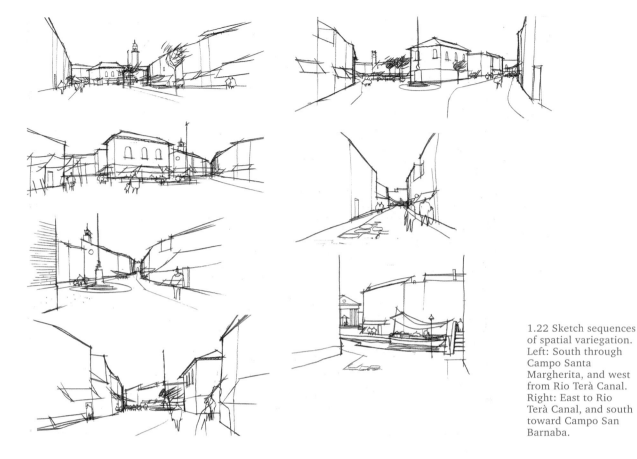

1.22 Sketch sequences of spatial variegation. Left: South through Campo Santa Margherita, and west from Rio Terà Canal. Right: East to Rio Terà Canal, and south toward Campo San Barnaba.

Sidebar: A Sequential Experience: Lost in the Labyrinth

The labyrinth of calli, vie, viali, salizzidi, fondamenti, etc., in conjunction with the correspondingly complex network of canals, defines the Venetian pedestrian experience, while the campi serve as knots or junctures in that web. A separate study could be made of this network of highly variegated and sometimes remarkably narrow passages. A taste of the experience it offers can be had by exiting Campo San Barnaba to the south and following the route which leads to Campo San Stefano. This sequence reveals some of the characteristics that transform what could otherwise be a straightforward byway of a couple of hundred yards into an experience of intrigue, disorientation, and surprise (Fig. 1.23).

A sottoportego in the south face of Campo San Barnaba, arcaded and masquerading as a building entrance, tunnels through to a gently curving fondamenta alongside a quiet rio (a). A zigzag discontinuity then winds the passage through a narrow gap alongside the water and into a seemingly dead-end byway (b). At its end, though, a left turn (c) reveals a long, straight section with a canal bridge at its end, a solid wall again terminating

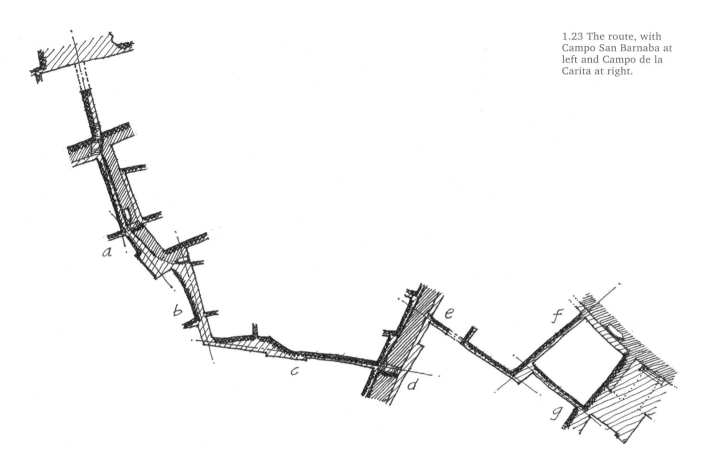

1.23 The route, with Campo San Barnaba at left and Campo de la Carita at right.

the vista (d). There, fondamenti reveal themselves extending in both directions on both sides of the bridge, the ubiquitous directional signs painted on streetscape walls becoming essential to know what to do next. A left turn across the bridge completes a disorienting disengagement from the localized grid of San Barnaba. A right turn (e) through another shadowy sottoportego leads to another blank wall beyond. A left turn again materializes, and a glimpse of the Grand Canal appears in the immediate distance (f). But since taking this appealing route leads to a dead end, a right turn should be taken, which frames a narrow view of monumental architecture and a glimpse of open space to come. There one enters, with a sudden expansion of scale and some relief for a renewed sense of orientation, the generous elbow of Campo de la Carita (g).

This very busy pavement accommodates a substantial frontage along the Grand Canal, a major vaporetto stop, the principal façade of the Gallerie dell'Accademia, and the south landing of the Accademia Bridge. The route just taken is somewhat atypical for Venice in that its disorienting twists and turns reflect, in part, a transition between two neighborhood grids. Despite often seeming a chaotic jumble, much of Venice is actually a stitched-together set of alignment zones. Distortions and rifts in geometry occur at the irregular transitions among these zones, resulting in a variety of such anomalies and captivating false alarms.

Sestiere San Marco: Campi de la Carita, San Vidal, San Stefano, & Sant'Angelo

Campo de la Carita and Campo San Vidal—the pavements linked by the Accademia Bridge—are a different category of urban open space: the dominating impact of the Grand Canal's broad swath casts them into a subordinate role, such that they are more in the nature of well-defined quaysides than urban squares (Fig. 1.24). Their other supporting role is as a part of the introductory procession leading to Campo San Stefano, Venice's most urbane and elegant square save San Marco itself. After the climb over the Grand Canal on

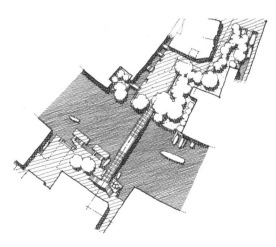

1.24 Ground Plan: Campo de la Carita (below) and Campo San Vidal (above).
The campi flank the Grand Canal, with the end of the preceding "labyrinth" at the bottom left and the entrance to Campo San Stefano at the top right. The spatial sequence is a series of doglegs, the expansive vistas of the Grand Canal contracting to narrow passages.

1.25 Looking north from the "zigzag" toward the first opening-up of Campo San Stefano.

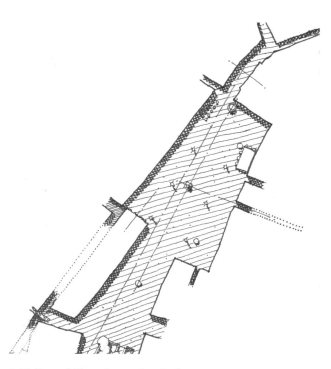

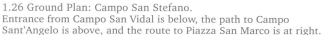
1.26 Ground Plan: Campo San Stefano.
Entrance from Campo San Vidal is below, the path to Campo
Sant'Angelo is above, and the route to Piazza San Marco is at right.

the Accademia, Campo San Vidal seems a bit of an anticlimax and, bafflingly, a dead end as well. But crowds emerging from the right rear corner give away yet another zigzag escape off the end of the space, as at Margherita and elsewhere, and this route follows the unusual overhanging luxuriance of a walled garden into Campo San Stefano itself.

In a further variant on the entry experience, this passage is gently deflected toward what appears to be simply a wider stretch of path ahead, disappearing into the distance past the flank of a church at the far end (Fig. 1.25). But the walled garden gives way to a room of space which opens up unexpectedly, only to neck back down before opening up, yet again, into the main body of the square (Figs. 1.26, 1.27). Centered on a rather uninteresting statue of Niccolò Tommaseo, the elongated arrowhead of the square sets up an unusual processional quality, reinforced by dual rows of ornate lanterns. The square, also known as Campo Francesco Morosini, has been described as "bourgeois" in character, in contrast to Santa Margherita's proletarian lack of

1.27 Looking north in Campo San Stefano, past the second "opening-up."
The square is now perceived as a two-to-one rectangle, though the barely perceptible convergence of the sidewalls subtly energizes the space and encourages further passage toward the far end. The route to Campo Sant'Angelo adjoins the sidewall of the Chiesa di San Stefano.

pretense.[10] With its mix of high-style and vernacular façades, languid café activity, and an absence of canals or trees within the space, San Stefano is almost austere in its urbanity.

The taut linear axis of Campo San Stefano points ultimately to a narrow passage, flanking the entrance to the 14th-century church itself, which leads in turn to an even narrower bending alleyway. Steps ahead confront another blind corner, mounting a bridge over a canal that skirts the near side of Campo Sant'Angelo, hidden from full view until the last corner is passed. (Fig. 1.28)[11] While only a few steps from San Stefano, this campo is not perceived as part of a continuous spatial sequence, as with Santa Margherita and San Barnaba, for the short sequence of narrow alleyways effects a complete separation.

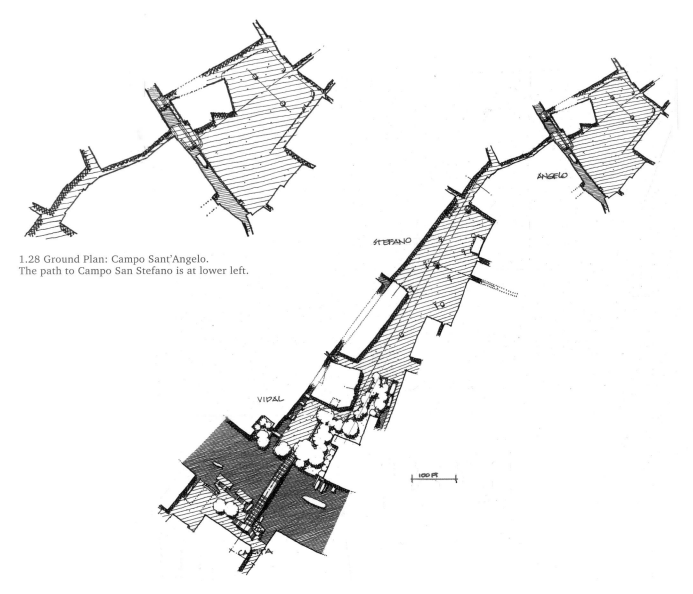

1.28 Ground Plan: Campo Sant'Angelo.
The path to Campo San Stefano is at lower left.

1.29 The combined sequence in plan centering on Campo San Stefano.

Campo Sant'Angelo ("San Anzolo" in the Venetian dialect) is more domestic in character than San Stefano, with a small open market operating at the far end in the morning. It presents another somewhat theatrical image, the sidewalls converging on the end wall, with the market fenced on three sides from aisles adjoining like a stage set on display. A freestanding building containing the tiny Oratory of the Annunciation screens the view of the approach from the alley and lends significant interest and ambiguity to the experience of the campo. It also serves as a pivot, swinging the perceived central axis around the blind corner and toward the center of the "stage" wall opposite, where a narrow calle reenters

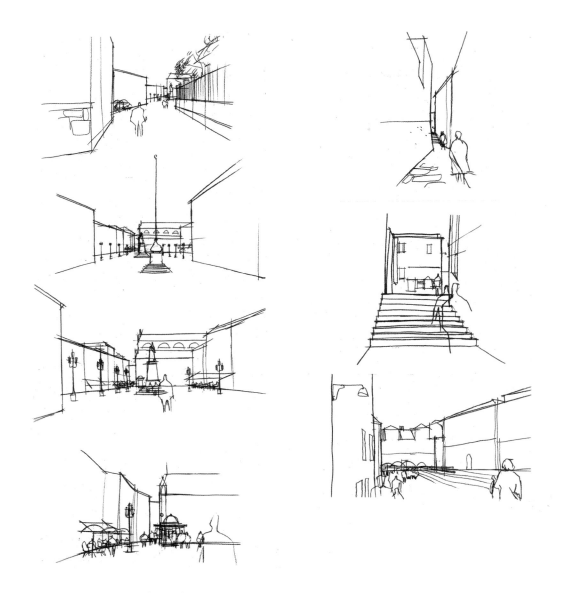

1.30 Sketch sequences of spatial variegation.
Left: Approaching Campo San Stefano from south; passing through San Stefano.
Right: Passage at the north end; entering Campo Sant'Angelo.

the labyrinth of central Venice. From there, an extended sequence of passages and smaller campi leads to the bustling vicinity of the Rialto Bridge at the Grand Canal. Although this northerly route to Sant'Angelo and beyond receives the full emphasis of San Stefano's arrowhead morphology, it is something of a red herring, for an insignificant mousehole to the east—one of several mere cracks in the sidewall fabric of San Stefano—leads to a more rewarding itinerary, the ever-crowded path to Piazza San Marco.

As with Campo Santa Margherita, two final figures give a sense of the preceding overall spatial sequence, showing the progression centering on Campo San Stefano in plan and in a series of sequential eye-level views (Figs. 1.29, 1.30).

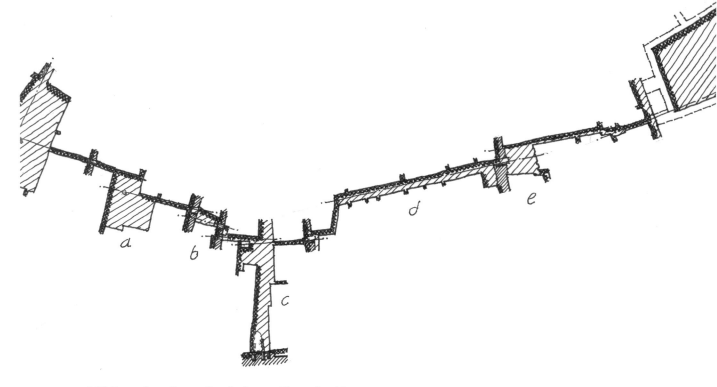

1.31 Route from Campo San Stefano to Piazza San Marco.

Sidebar: A Sequential Experience: Streets & Squares

While some connective routes are too extended to form a memorably integrated sequence, the route from Campo San Stefano to Piazza San Marco is an object lesson in the effective alternation of narrow passages and understated squares (Fig. 1.31).[12] Close by Campo San Stefano, Campo San Maurizio (a) is rectangular and plain, followed by tiny Campiello de la Feltrina, (b) featuring complex stepped bridges. Campo Santa Maria Zobenigo (c) extrudes down to a glimpse of the Grand Canal. Linking passages slip in and out of the corners of these spaces, with localized axialities lending a subtext of order to the otherwise picturesque sequences. A different spatial experience follows: the unusually broad, straight Calle Largo XXII Marzo (d) stretches out to terminate on axis with the Campo San Moisé (e) and its church façade in an uncharacteristic ensemble of classical symmetry. Of this church Ruskin wrote "it is notable as one of the basest examples of the basest schools of the Renaissance" and it's hard to disagree.[13] Narrow passages exiting at both sides of this clumsy pile make a game of wayfinding, with one leading basically nowhere, while the other emerges, shortly and with little fanfare, at Piazza San Marco.

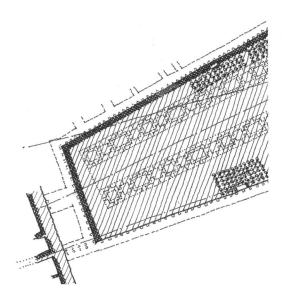

1.32 Ground Plan West: Piazza San Marco.
Note the corner entrance, obtuse-angled corner,
and off-center pavement axis.

1.33 Piazza San Marco: View to east at entry.
View in at the arcaded southwest corner entrance, the terminus
of the route from Campo San Stefano. The entry axis aligns with
the gap defined by the campanile and ends at a glimpse of the
Doge's Palace.

Sestiere San Marco: Piazza San Marco & the Piazzetta

From this approach, Piazza San Marco is entered in a characteristically understated fashion, by slipping in at a rear corner through an inconspicuous underpass. In most other respects, the Piazza is very much an exception to the way the urban open spaces of Venice work. Some of its notable features are well known, such as the fact that the Piazza itself is a trapezoid which angles markedly off the basilica's axis, or that two quite different "tapestries" of sidewall treatment join in abrupt misalignment at one corner. The campanile is an axle anchoring the ultimate center of Venice, about which the spatial ensemble of the Piazza and Piazzetta revolves, its mass necking down the junctures between them to provide both spatial definition and counterpoint. The axialized view into the Piazza from this western approach slides neatly through the gap beside the campanile (Figs. 1.32, 1.33).

Entry from the north, via the crowded, narrow shopping street of the mercerias, focuses on a glimpse of the open space beyond, through the base of the Torre dell'Orologio. Once in the open, the flanking sidewalls—the real one of the Basilica di San Marco and the phantom

wall defined by three flagpoles—neck down in false perspective to the next "portal," defined by the campanile. There the space reopens into the Piazzetta, only to focus down once again, the footprint of this recursive sequence recalling that of Campo San Stefano (Figs. 1.34, 1.35). Pavement runners point to the paired columns which are the grand exception to the Venetian tradition of secret little entries, framing the Piazzetta's portal to (and from) the Bacino. The apparition of Palladio's San Giorgio Maggiore across the water is not quite the axial terminus of this linear progression, for the island church and the flanking tip of the Giudecca define a final portal, the Canale

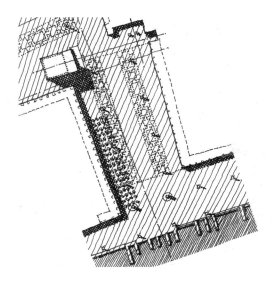

1.34 Ground Plan: The Piazzetta.
Note the several primary and secondary axial alignments.

1.35 The Piazzetta: View to south.
View to the Bacino, flanked by the Columns of San Marco and San Teodoro. The island of San Giorgio Maggiore (the church façade clad in scaffolding) and the islands of the Giudecca flank the Canale della Grazia, with the lagoon beyond and the Lido in the distance. Open at both ends, the Piazzetta can seems more a grand hallway than a salon, despite its magisterial proportions.

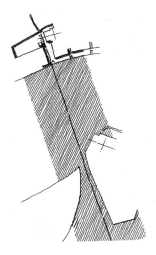
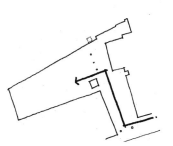
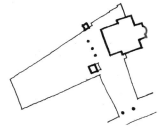
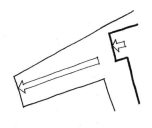

1.36a Axis from Piazza San Marco to the Lido.
1.36b Zigzag Entry to Piazza San Marco.

1.37a Foreground Elements in Piazza San Marco and the Piazzetta.
1.37b Analogous Forms of the Piazza and the Basilica di San Marco.

della Grazia, which opens to the lagoon beyond and the faintly visible Lido in the distance (Fig. 1.36a). So the underlying reality of Venice's centerpiece spatial axis makes perfect if not terribly appealing sense, with shopping and gambling as the two poles, processing en route past monuments of religion, art, culture, and government.

While the columns mark a grand water axis befitting what was once a mighty port, the entry sequence from quayside is more characteristically eccentric: approaching along the magisterial arc of the Riva degli Schiavoni, one perceives the paired columns not as a portal but as another phantom defining wall, working with the flank of the Doge's Palace to funnel the spatial route around the corner. Another zigzag blind entry results, with the Piazzetta revealed only as the corner is reached. Thanks in large part to the campanile, a similarly veiled approach is then made to the Piazza (Fig. 1.36b).

In addition to being the largest defined open spaces in Venice and marking the hub of power for church and state, the Piazza and Piazzetta have a uniformity of boundary treatment which is completely different from the campi. While the arcaded sidewalls are highly developed with elaborate detail, the overall impression is of a regularized brocade-like backdrop, confident but unassertive. An irregular composition of special elements—the Basilica, the Torre dell'Orologio, the campanile, the columns—acts as the foreground for this backdrop, and each element has its part to play (Fig. 1.37a). The interaction among these elements and the spatial boundaries results in the inimitable qualities which render this urban experience one of the most admired in the world.

The remarkable uniformity of the Piazza's three contiguous sides seems a perfect foil for this interplay of foreground elements, but this happy result did, of course, evolve over centuries. The pair of iconic restaurants facing each other along the sides, with their sunshades, bandstands, and arrays of tables, seems just the right degree of exception to the rule of uniformity. While seeming self-evidently right to us today, it bears noting that the large bulk of the ground floors defining the Piazza and Piazzetta are indeed devoted to such cafés and other public functions

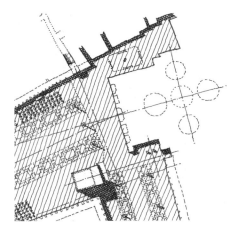

1.38 Ground Plan East: Piazza San Marco.
Clockwise from top: Torre dell'Orologio (at entrance from north); Piazzetta dei Leoni; Basilica di San Marco; Entry to Piazzetta; the Campanile.

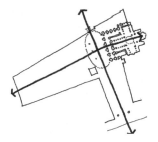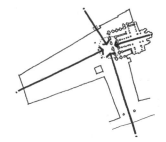

1.39a The Piazza and Piazzetta as a crossroads.
1.39b The Piazza and Piazzetta as a convergence of radials.

which visually and physically activate the campi, while landmark entities such as the Museo Correr, the Venice offices of the Italian President, and the National Library are relegated to upper floors. Another fact of great significance, which may not be consciously noted by many of its throngs of tourists, is that Piazza San Marco is one of the few great urban spaces in Europe where human voices prevail over the sounds of motorized traffic.

The projecting porch and nave of the Basilica act in conjunction with the volume of the Doge's Palace to form an L-shaped volume, analogous in form to the more elongated elbow of open space that it helps to define. This relationship, with the Piazza extending out in seeming response to the Basilica's assertive projection, is an important element in the dynamic impression made by the ensemble (Fig. 1.37b). The campanile serves not only to nail down this dynamic sweep and mutually define and screen the spaces, but to visually buttress the potentially weak definition where the sidewall of the Procuratie Nuove turns the corner (Fig. 1.38). The foursquare campanile has an appended entry element at its base, the

Loggetta, which further necks down and defines the portal gap between the two great squares, as well as answering the recess opposite where the Doge's Palace meets the basilica and gives access to its courtyard. This juncture of spaces and volumes is made richer yet by a pair of freestanding square columns centered on a bay of the basilica's south façade, brought from Constantinople after the Fourth Crusade, which subtly establish their own subsidiary longitudinal axis through the Piazzetta.

One way to read the ensemble of the Piazza and Piazzetta is as a crossroads (Fig. 1.39a). In the case of the Piazza, its axial experience does not end at the Basilica, but focuses processional attention onto entry into the church. The basilica interior, itself an axial sequence of narthex, nave, crossing, choir, and apse in the Western tradition, continues and completes this procession. In turn, the perpendicular axis of the Piazzetta is demarked by its two portals, the columns, and the Orologio. The zone where these two axial spaces cross, bounded by flagpoles, Basilica, Orologio, and campanile, is highly charged

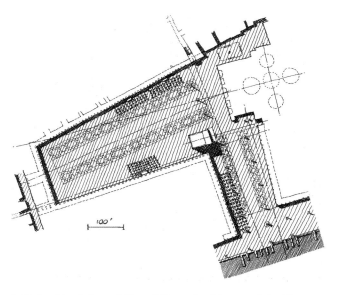

1.40 Combined Ground Plan of Piazza San Marco and the Piazzetta.

by the formal and spatial energies of all these forces.

This spatial order can also be perceived as radial in nature, with the Piazza, Piazzetta, and Orologio passage converging at the Basilica's center door (Fig. 1.39b). A fourth radial axis reinforces the pattern, for just as the Basilica entrance draws worshipers and tourists in toward the sequential goals of its interior, a recessional dynamic reverses this order, leaving by the central western door and meeting the other three paths: an urban confluence of "sacred and profane."

Some final images represent the combined ensemble of the Piazza San Marco and the Piazzetta—in plan; from within; and as seen from the Bacino di San Marco (Figs. 1.40, 1.41, 1.42).

1.41 Piazza San Marco: View to east.

1.42 View from the Bacino di San Marco. Left to right: Giardini Reali; the Libreria and Procurate Nuove; the Campanile; the two columns marking the entrance to the Piazzetta, with the Piazza San Marco, the Torre dell'Orologio and the Basilica di San Marco glimpsed beyond; and the Doge's Palace, with the "Bridge of Sighs."

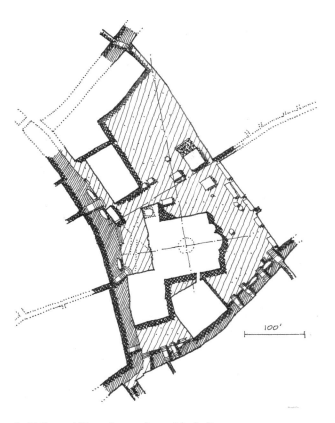

1.43 Ground Plan: Campo Santa Maria Formosa.

Sestiere Castello: Campo Santa Maria Formosa

Although the nearest to San Marco of these campi, Campo Santa Maria Formosa is isolated by dense intervening urban fabric. The ensemble's footprint shows superficial similarities to another aspect of San Giacomo, in that a waterfront entry campiello at the church leads through a portal-like narrows into the much larger main space. But it is the differences which merit scrutiny. Treeless and too big for the life it accommodates—mainly as a market square in the morning—the campo ends up with empty space in its corners and lacking a sense of focus, its crossroads of pedestrian routes further hindering a sense of place (Figs. 1.43, 1.44).[14]

The variety of styles and periods that line the campo help out to some extent, being lively while also remarkably homogenous and coherent, but the church is the campo's best feature, a commanding and muscular presence boldly intruding to provide spatial intrigue for its half of the symmetrically bifurcated square (Fig. 1.45). Scraps of space find their way back around it to the eastern canal, and another waterway edges the south flank with a crowded stitching of bridges. But since these bridges lead directly into the sidewall of the space with no opposite embankment, this canal seems to clutter and weaken the space rather than affording a welcome amenity as at San Barnaba. Although canals closely

1.44 Campo Santa
Maria Formosa: View to
north.
Tall sidewalls,
variegated façades
and the commanding
church define the
campo, but they are
insufficient to enliven
its large expanse
of uninterrupted
pavement. Routes from
Piazza San Marco and
Campo San Zanipolo
enter from left and
right respectively, the
latter, a virtual crack
in the sidewall at the
slight step-in.

1.45 Campo Santa Maria Formosa: View to south.

adjoin three sides of the campo, making it more nearly an island than almost any other major square, the ironic prevailing impression is rather dry, an island of hard-edged half-emptiness in its teeming matrix of urban fabric.

The volume of the church is indeed a bravura spacemaking element, comprising the focus of the square and the source of its several aspects of spatial interest. The space of the campo per se is, in fact, a remarkably precise parallelogram, thus depending significantly on the church and its forecourt for variegation. While the church's ceremonial entry faces the adjoining Fondamenta della Chiesa, its side exposure commands a long diagonal view of the campo itself and is developed as an assertive entry ensemble, in effect a true second front entrance for the church which incorporates a witty byplay of baroque motifs and elements.

The church's commanding tower acts as a pivot marking the transition between the campo and the fondamenta, recalling San Marco's campanile in this respect and conveniently framing both façades simultaneously. As a further nicety of spatial transition, a modest one-story structure flanking the canal stops the axis through this gap, pleasantly complicating the sequential relationship by forcing a rotation into the adjoining fondamenta. Only then is the canal embankment that is denied the campo itself finally revealed, aligned as a negative backdrop to the positive focus of the church's ceremonial façade.

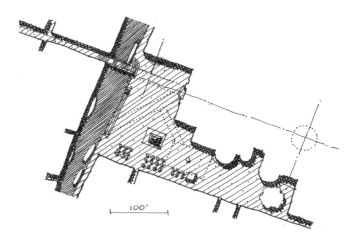

1.46 Ground Plan: Campo Santi Giovanni e Paolo, often called Campo San Zanipolo.
The via at the upper left leads to Campo Santa Maria Nova. The Scuola Grande di San Marco is at the top center.

Sestiere Castello: Campo Santi Giovanni e Paolo

A final pair of campi are somewhat less well-known than many of the above, yet they epitomize what the squares of Venice can tell us today about humane urban space, and provide an apt summary of the campi's best elements and qualities.

Campo Santi Giovanni e Paolo (often conflated to "San Zanipolo" in the Venetian dialect) is something of a palimpsest, bringing together aspects of several other squares in an ensemble that also has its own unique qualities (Fig. 1.46). As at San Giacomo and Santa Maria Formosa, assertive church volumes face a flattened yet variegated urban backcloth. But this square also does the Campi dei Frari and San Barnaba one better in its role as an

1.47 Campo Santi Giovanni e Paolo: View to west.
The space expands toward the intensely varied façades across
the canal, which echo the long array of the south perimeter. This
elbow of the roughly L-shaped campo contrasts with the more
monolithic and monumental façades of the Basilica di Santi
Giovanni e Paolo and the Scuola Grande di San Marco.

impressive church forecourt. And, as at
San Barnaba and San Pantalon, the church
façade competes for attention with a
bustling canal frontage, here featuring an
expansive stretch of landing. The church—
the Basilica dei Santi Giovanni e Paolo—
competes as well with the adjoining stage-
set-like entrance façade of the Scuola
Grande di San Marco, recalling the dueling
façades of Campo San Rocco, but here
there is sufficient space, differentiation,
and focus to accommodate them both.
Verrocchio's equestrian Colleoni statue,
raised to a skyline silhouette on its
massive pedestal, provides that focus,
anchoring the L-shaped space at its elbow
(Figs. 1.47, 1.48).

1.48 Façade of Scuola Grande di San Marco, facing south to
Campo Santi Giovanni e Paolo.
The façade of the Scuola—not to be confused with the Basilica
di San Marco—addresses the minor axis of this campo, while
the abutting entry façade of the Basilica dei Santi Giovanni e
Paolo addresses the route to the campo that follows.

51

The campo narrows down to a completely different experience at the opposite end, with an intimate scale matched by a bucolic ensemble of trees and benches (Fig. 1.49). There is something appealingly contrary about the way this spatial compression leads not to some climactic gesture but to a restful byway, serving as a valuable contrast to the assertive ensemble at the other end. Elongated arrays of café tables reinforce the backbone of the south wall and afford a stretched-out audience for these urbanistic theatrics. Engaging though the square is, its elongated and stepping-out qualities tend to undercut its sense of place, and the monumental scale of the church, while less overwhelming than the Frari, adds to the imbalance. The square's greatest success is as a lively backdrop for commanding façades.

1.49 Campo Santi Giovanni e Paolo: View to east.
In the opposite direction, the side chapels of the basilica have compressed and helped define this end of the campo into the contrasting experience of an intimately scaled and restful retreat.

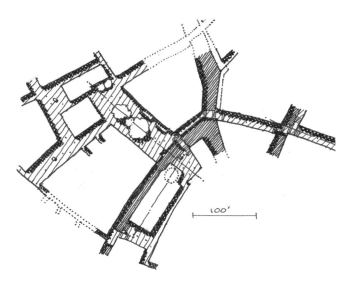

1.50 Ground Plan: Campo Santa Maria Nova. The campo is left of the center, with adjoining campielli shown. The church of Santa Maria dei Miracoli is at the bottom center.

Sestiere Cannaregio: Campo Santa Maria Nova

On axis with the Zanipolo church, in an unusual case of symmetrical alignment, a bridge adjoining the Scuola leads across the canal to an eastward link toward Campo Santa Maria Nova (Fig. 1.50). The connection is *almost* direct, enough so that the two campi can be experienced sequentially, yet with a crucial complication as the end is approached. A bridge leads to an abrupt bend in the path in a watery region of rich ambiguity, for the canal as well as the volumes that define it keep changing, exhibiting a lack of consistent structure that is unusual even for Venice. This intriguing set-piece of curving, colliding waterways and pointed, sheared, and jumbled volumes suddenly resolves with effective contrast into the orderly space of Campo Santa Maria Nova. Its spatial footprint is rectangular, simpler on the face of it than any of the other squares discussed save San Barnaba, and almost all its periphery consists of plainspoken urban sidewall with no particular architectural embellishment.

Yet there are several factors which lend this modest square a timeless quality that makes it memorable. To a degree

1.51 Campo Santa Maria Nova: View to northwest.
The sidewalls, while variegated, are not especially interesting, but they are tall in proportion to the small scale of the campo and help give it a well-defined, room-like character.

otherwise unprecedented among these squares, it is surrounded by a nearly contiguous ring of circumferential passages and subsidiary spaces, a circulatory "halo" which lends an enhanced sense of arrival and focus to the square itself. Secondly, a picturesque grouping of trees, benches, and café umbrellas occupies the center of the square (Fig. 1.51). This is somewhat unusual among these campi, and here the space's intimate proportions lend this ensemble an importance which enlarges one's experience, entwined with the characteristic diagonal routes taken by pedestrians and effectively populating and activating the space. Finally, there is the aggregation of elements at the square's southeast end, where the through-passing

canal isolates a small pocket of pavement, flanked by the projecting apse of the church of Santa Maria dei Miracoli (Fig. 1.52).[15] This monument of blazing white, gray, and yellow marble is gentled and rendered more believable by partially obscuring tree cover. A pronounced theatrical quality prevails yet again, with the ditch of the canal as orchestra pit and the apsidal campiello a stage, its fantasy stage set of the Miracoli moving in from the wings, its feet in the water. The audience sits in a space the shape of an intimate music hall, enjoying the intermission.

1.52 Campo Santa Maria Nova: View to southeast. The entrance coming from Campo San Zanipolo at the left, and the impressive apse of Santa Maria dei Miracoli at the right, define the focused pocket of space that lends a theatrical quality to the composition of the campo.

2 Other Notes on the Campi and Environs

Daily Life in the Campi

The islands that make up Venice were once semi-autonomous, with houses built around the edges, accessing the water directly for transportation and commerce. The campo—the central open space—was used for community needs such as grazing cattle, festivals, and markets, resulting in a strong sense of neighborhood rivalry and identity. Paved paths developed for crossing the otherwise grassy open spaces, leading eventually to the all-but-fully-paved spaces seen today.

It seems clear that the campi were indeed the communal living rooms of their neighborhoods, frequented both by those residing nearby and those passing through on their way to work, leading to a rich interplay of social interaction. A map's eye view reveals that, while the privileged had private gardens to enjoy, many residents did not, depending on the inadequate resources of narrow vias or small areaways for natural light, outlook, and ventilation. These cases reinforce the important community role of the campi in the daily life of the city and its citizens.

In modern times tourism has clearly grown to become a source of problems for Venice, which include overcrowding, noise, and litter. Even Piazza San Marco's capacity can seem strained, suffering the impact of crowds released from huge cruise ships. Tourism is a double-edged sword for Venice, affording an economic boon, but causing an ongoing exodus of citizens to the mainland. Campi that are not far from the Piazza, such as San Stefano and Santa Maria Formosa, also show evidence of significantly large numbers of pedestrians and restaurant patrons in recent decades. But even though the effects of tourism are now felt throughout the islands of Venice, it remains the case that more isolated and lesser known campi such as San Giacomo, San Polo, and Santa Maria Nova still retain some semblance of their roles as living centers for their neighborhoods.

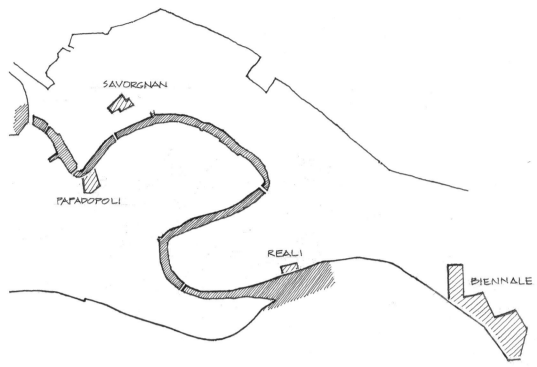

2.1 Locations of Venice's Public Gardens.

Rus in Urbe

A striking aspect of all these squares is the predominance of "hardscape." Plant material on the ground plane is sparse, when present at all, and trees occur in limited groupings, sometimes emerging from pavement receptors without recourse to foundation plantings. This is the typical paradigm of urban open spaces in Mediterranean towns, and indeed largely the case throughout Europe. Clearly, limited landscape is simpler to maintain, and extensive open pavements afford a maximum of flexibility for intermittently occurring events such as markets, performances, and festivals, not to mention for routes of pedestrian crossings. Beyond such functional issues, though, one ponders the question of the plausible desirability of incorporating landscape into the city. "Rus in urbe" is a pertinent phrase generally meaning an illusion of countryside created by a building or garden within a city, evoking a haven of peace and quiet within an urban setting. Le Corbusier and Frank Lloyd Wright, in their own differently flawed visions, sought a sort of complete integration of Rus and Urbe, with naturalistically treated open space flowing among individually sited structures. The generally conceded fallacy of those visions is the lack of sequence or definition, notwithstanding the overarching fact that cities, to this day, stubbornly seek high densities.

Thinking through urban open space precedents of both Europe and America, we often, of course, have both: green squares and paved ones. But the green square (or park, mall, or greenway) is notably a "haven of peace and quiet" as opposed to the bustling activity of the paved plaza: not of the same faith and order as these Venetian squares. Modest American county seats will often feature the courthouse centered on a block of lawn and trees but, pleasant as they may be, these are not particularly well-defined urban open spaces. We don't, in fact, have a particularly well-defined tradition of town squares in the USA.

Venice does have many verdant, leafy spaces, but you wouldn't know it walking the byways, for most are behind walls: private gardens, glimpsed through barred gates or suggested by greenery extending over. There are but four public gardens in Venice proper: the Giardino Papadopoli near the railroad station, the Giardini Reali around the corner from the Piazza San Marco, the Giardini della Biennale in Castello, and, a bit more hidden, the Parco Savorgnan in Cannaregio, once a private garden (Fig. 2.1). Venice's ubiquitous paved campi—seldom without some greenery of their own—are the urban complement to these gardens.

2.2a Piazza San Marco's sidewall uniformity.

Sidewalls

While these comments have focused on such issues as spatial sequence, entry, and the disposition of elements, they have not dealt very much with the "eye-level experience" of the sidewalls of the campi. But is it reasonable to look to the long-evolved urban fabric of another culture and time in a search for useful observations about urban space in the modern age, particularly when it comes to more specific façade issues? While some things have changed a great deal, a lot has not changed very much: if we can't find something useful in a searching look at one of the most beautiful cities in the world, we aren't trying very hard.

The characteristics of the campo sidewalls (Piazza San Marco again being an exception to these generalities) are surprisingly consistent. While virtually contiguous, they are highly varied as to skyline, floor line, number of floors, and fenestration (Figs. 2.2a & b). Extents of the same treatment are interrupted at felicitous junctures by more colorful exceptions. They are flat, vertical surfaces that firmly establish the boundaries of the outdoor room, embellished and enhanced by elements such as balconies and grouped openings that often establish zones of localized symmetry.

Ground floors are highly variegated, incorporating modern storefronts, contrasting sections of solid sidewall, and all variations between. They are of modest means with simple materials dominating, special treatments being limited to exceptional elements or focal point structures. The level of detail interest embodied in the campo sidewalls is characterized by "fractal scalability": the eye is engaged by interesting and appropriate visual incident across all scales. The campo sidewalls have evolved, subtly yet effectively, to serve the outdoor rooms of the city—the foyers, salons, dining rooms and play spaces—that they define.

2.2b Campo San Stefano's sidewall variegation.

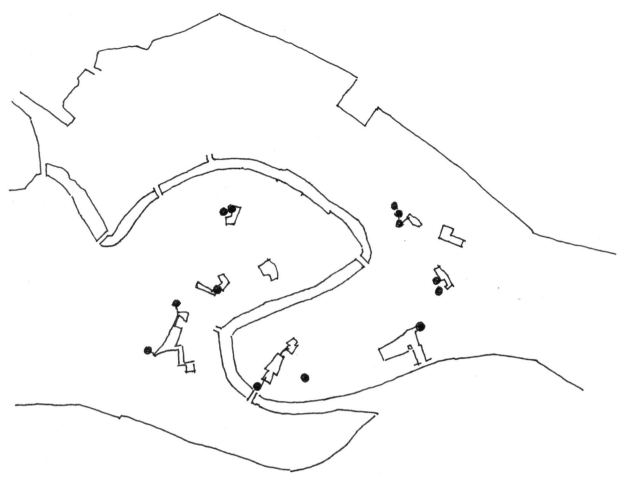

2.3 Locations of the Campielli discussed.

Campielli

Many campi act in consort with *campielli,* which are also well-defined urban spaces but on a smaller scale (Fig. 2.3). A closer look at these little squares reveals the important role they play as "tenders" for campi, as well as other ways they take part in and enhance the sequential experience of Venice. There is a rich continuum of roles played by the campielli, ranging from direct continuity with other urban spaces to complete isolation in the urban labyrinth.

Contiguous

At one extreme, small subsidiary spaces are separated from a major space merely by an angled orientation or a narrowed juncture; as such, they are immediate enhancements to the spatial experience of the campo (Fig. 2.4). At Campo San Giacomo, Campiello dei Morti is a contiguous alcove of the main space set off by the projecting mass of the church, readily perceived as part and parcel of the overall space while also having some degree of spatial identity of its own and demonstrating the pleasurable ambiguities that obtain when one space becomes another. The small space beyond Campo dei Frari along Calle Tintoretto, very much

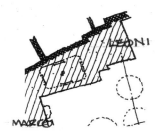

2.4 Ground Plans: Contiguous campielli.

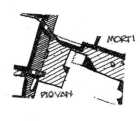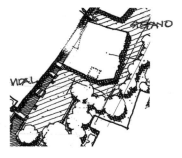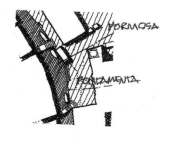

2.5 Ground Plans: Linked campielli.

like a campiello, also plays this role, by virtue of being wholly visible to the campo yet having its own more intimate identity. The grandeur of Piazza San Marco itself eclipses another smaller contiguous space, Piazzetta dei Leoni, defined by the north side of the Basilica. Named for its two large stone sculptures of lions, the space serves to help set off the Basilica and, as above, to add character and scale variegation to the overall spatial experience of the Piazza and Piazzetta.

Linked

By virtue of more defined separation, some campielli retain close adjacencies as forecourts to campi while fully becoming urban spaces on their own accord (Fig. 2.5). Adjoining Campo San Giacomo to the west, the canal-flanked Campiello dei Piovan links with the larger space through a narrow neck, with further expansion and transition to follow as one moves into Campiello dei Morti and the rest of this U-shaped campo.

A similar experience prevails at Campo San Vidal at the north landing of the Accademia Bridge, where the short link to Campo San Stefano beyond is enhanced by its blind corner; once the corner is turned the remaining leg faces directly up the axis of the campo, as in the cases above. And adjacent to Campo Santa Maria Formosa, Fondamenta della Chiesa again presents a modest space facing a canal, with a linking neck which affords just enough separation to maintain the individual identity of the two spaces. Thus these Janus-faced campielli have it both ways, serving as foyers to the linked campi yet also able to stand on their own merits. Further, they have two special features in common that enhance the differentiation of the paired spaces while reinforcing their linkage: towers located at the pivot points of connection serve the latter purpose, nailing down and demarking the juncture of each ensemble, while each campiello also features substantial canal frontage, a distinctive feature enhancing its contrast with the "dry" campo adjoining.

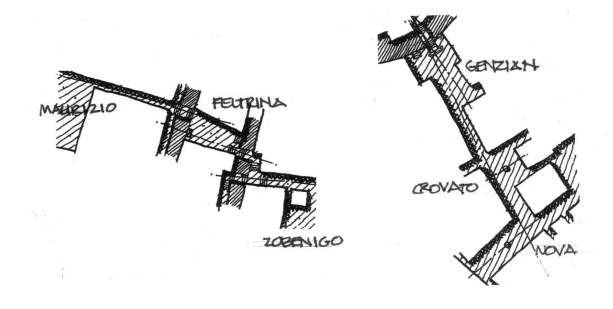

2.6 Ground Plans: Sequenced campielli.

Sequenced

While in the above cases the campielli are ganged symbiotically with individual campi, they may also act in linked sequence with several other larger and smaller spaces like variegated beads on a chain (Fig. 2.6). Campiello de la Feltrina, tucked between Campo San Maurizio and Campo Santa Maria Zobenigo on the "streets and squares" route to Piazza San Marco, serves a small-scaled but pivotal role in this richly varied sequence. And in proximity to Campo Santa Maria Nova, three small spaces—Campielli Santa Maria Nova, San Crovato, and San Genzian—are linked by short connectors in a captivating sequence.

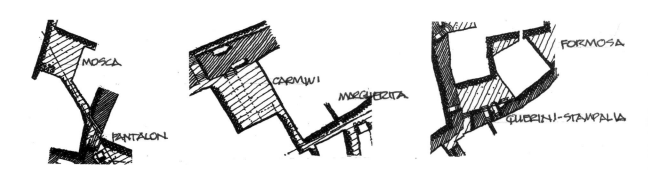

2.7 Ground Plans: Separated campielli.

Separated

Spatial connectivity is all a matter of degree: a combined function of the length of the separation, the narrowness of the link, and bends that may obstruct sightlines. Combinations of these factors and others can mean that a campiello seems spatially independent despite close proximity to other spaces (Fig. 2.7). Such is the case of Campiello Mosca, so near and yet so far from the bustle of Campo San Pantalon. Campiello Carmini is just around the corner from Campo Santa Margherita, but there is little perceived connection. And in addition to Fondamenta della Chiesa, Campo Santa Maria Formosa features a second directly adjoining small square, Campiello Querini-Stampalia, but a narrow and angled connection renders it a completely distinct and separate experience. In these cases, physical proximity means there is a high likelihood of passing from one space to the other, but the geometry of separation defuses any perception of spatial sequence, and the resulting experiences benefit from mutual contrast and surprise.

The Campi as a Matrix of Spatial Types

By taking some liberties with both relative scale and handedness, issues of form variegation and proportion can generate an intriguing matrix among the campi (Fig. 2.8):

- Campo San Barnaba, the base case of a nearly true square, leads to Campo Santa Maria Nova with its rectangular proportions.
- When projections gradually intrude into these elemental shapes, spatial intrigue is enhanced, as in Campi San Polo and San Zanipolo, while larger such "intrusions" define Campi dei Frari and Santa Maria Formosa.
- Corresponding progressions of increasing attenuation lead to "arrowhead" distortions, as at Campi San Stefano and San Rocco.
- A final step in these progressions reveals a loss of coherence as single spaces, as in the linked spaces of Piazza San Marco and the Piazzetta, Campo San Giacomo, and finally the sweeping ambiguity of Campo Santa Margherita.

The resulting array offers some insight into several continua of spatial approaches, all of which are of value depending on the spatial and functional issues that a particular space addresses.

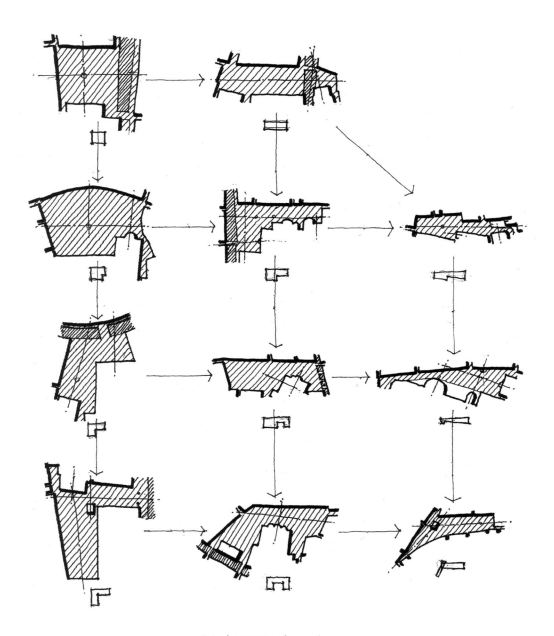

2.8 The Matrix of spatial types.

3 Findings

Many assertions can be made as to what aspects may be good or ill for the success of an urban open space, and variables of culture, climate, and program make useful generalizations challenging. But within the Western tradition, the Venetian squares seem a pertinent and inspiring laboratory in which to search for insights (Fig. 3.1). The above observations on these squares can be usefully condensed into a series of "recommendations to consider": straightforward and demonstrated strategies for the crafting of lively, intriguing, and fitting urban public spaces, which follow.

Sequenced Entry

Fittingly, aspects of approach and entry into a space come first among these findings. Entry into a significant defined urban space can often benefit from a "preliminary" preparatory experience, something more than simply passing a point where a linear street-like space opens out into a room-like space. Such a gesture may be called a forecourt, analogous to a narthex in a church or the lobby of an auditorium. Smaller in scale than the defined space that lies next in sequence, such a forecourt is more than an alcove-like appendage, with a well-defined perimeter and character of its own. It is of interest, yet subsidiary to and preparatory for the larger experience to follow, as at Campi San Giacomo and Santa Maria Formosa (Fig. 3.2). When approached from the Riva degli Schiavoni, the Piazzetta is itself such a forecourt for the Piazza San Marco.

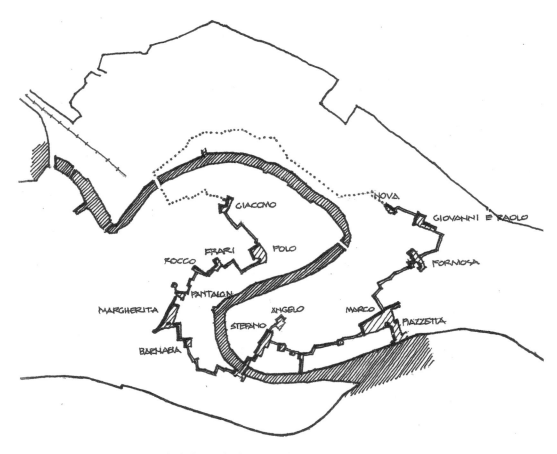

3.1 The selected campi as a linked chain of urban experiences.

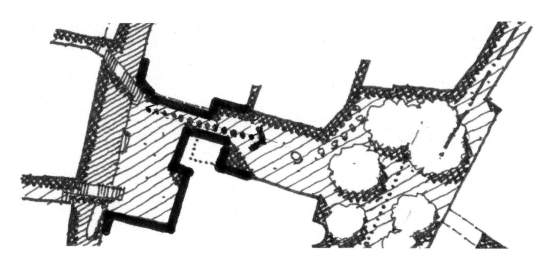

3.2 Sequenced entry: Campiello dei Piovan serves as a forecourt to Campiello dei Morti and, ultimately, to Campo San Giacomo.

Obscured View in at Entry

Whether or not such a forecourt is involved, an "obscuring" of the entry experience in one or another of several ways can be effective and dramatic. Recalling the Japanese tradition of indirection, the intent is to withhold revealing very much about the nature of the square until actual entry is achieved, in order to enhance the desirable aspects of surprise, intrigue, and interest. The simplest case finds a narrow, linear passage *aligning* directly with entry into the square, the excerpted view of its interior being so limited that the goal of delay is achieved. The very narrowness of the passage renders entry all the more impressive. Among others, this treatment appears at Campi San Giacomo, Santa Margherita, and San Zanipolo. By moving the entry passage to a corner of the space, the limitation of view is increased, and more so when employing the time-honored approach of *deflecting* or curving the sidewall beyond the entry point, which we have seen on approaching entry to Campi San Polo, dei Frari, and San Rocco (Fig. 3.3).

Further variations on this theme of obscured entry include "zigzagging" the entry passage to add a bit of obscuring labyrinth to a link between two spaces. This occurs at a large scale where the Piazzetta itself is a dogleg link between the Riva degli Schiavoni and Piazza San Marco. Other, smaller such doglegs link Campi Santa Margherita to San Barnaba and San Vidal to San Stefano.

An elaboration on this treatment involves an intervening obstruction, which encourages a *bypassing* route and a turn or "tee" junction, as at Campo Santa Margherita and Piazza San Marco—the Piazza's obscuring element being the campanile. A final variation involves a roofed or arcaded entry passage, or a sottoportego-like entry *tunneling* through a perimeter building, further necking down the excerpt of the space that is visible on approach. Different versions of this are seen at Campi San Polo and San Barnaba, and at Piazza San Marco (Fig. 3.4).

"Antonyms" to these strategies—practices which would defeat the delay in revealing a spatial experience that we are considering an often-desirable goal—would consist of broad axes of approach, revealing the nature of the square well before the point of entry. As to the particular case of obstructing the view in on approach with a turning or zigzag path, a clear antithesis would be a "neoclassical" axis of continuity, extending through the space to exit on axis at the other end, doing harm to the integrity of the space in its presumed role as a locale of activity by giving emphasis to a through-passing axial passage (Fig. 3.5).

View in at Entry, Obscured from Within

As a sub-variant of the zigzag entry, the square itself sometimes has an elbow-like configuration which truncates the view in, limiting it to a subset of the space until full entry is achieved— another way to delay the full reveal of the square. This characteristic situation is found at Campi Sant'Angelo and San Zanipolo. Such obscuring from within can also arise from the nature and contents of the square itself. Freestanding structures, groupings of trees, and the like will have a layering and screening effect that adds ambiguity and richness to a space, if it has a multifaceted and multifunctional nature that would render this desirable. Campo Santa Margherita, the market square, would be the foremost exemplar of this case (Fig. 3.6).

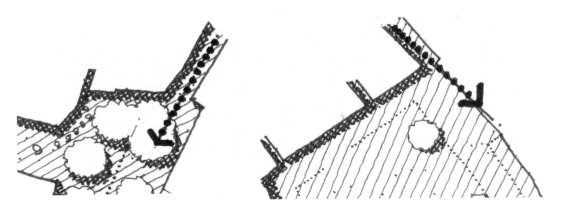

3.3 Obscured views in: narrow at San Giacomo; deflected at San Polo.

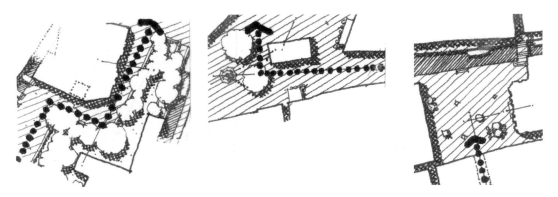

3.4 Obscured views in: zigzagged at San Stefano; bypassing at Santa Margherita; tunnel-like at San Barnaba.

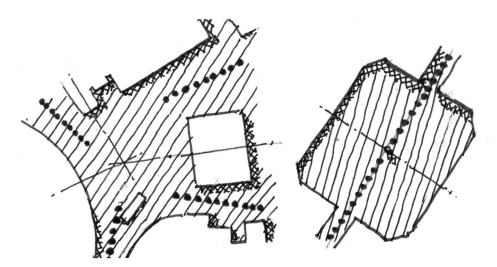

3.5 Antonyms: Boston's City Hall Plaza, ostensibly inspired by Siena's Piazza del Campo, has wide-open spatial connections in all directions. Paris' bisymmetrical Place Vendome, a trafficway rather than a place for people, has a through-passing cross axis marked by its only distinctive element, a central war memorial column.

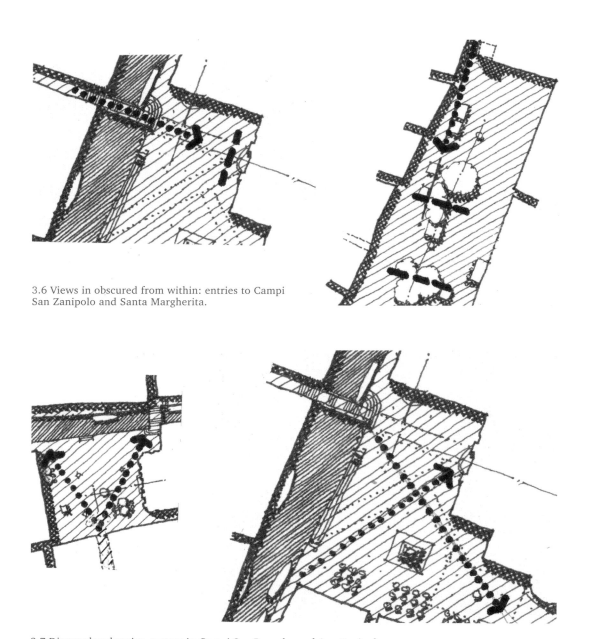

3.6 Views in obscured from within: entries to Campi San Zanipolo and Santa Margherita.

3.7 Diagonal pedestrian routes: in Campi San Barnaba and San Zanipolo.

Diagonal Routes Through

As opposed to a "through passing" axial pedestrian route, diagonal routes through a square will enliven it by virtue both of their skewed relationship to the space's boundaries and by defining varied and irregular subsections of the square's footprint for activity or repose (Fig. 3.7). They will occur as a matter of course if entry points are placed at or near the corners of a square, pursuant to the goal of obscured entry. Such cases are more the norm than the exception among the campi, occurring at Campi San Polo, San Barnaba, San Zanipolo, and others.

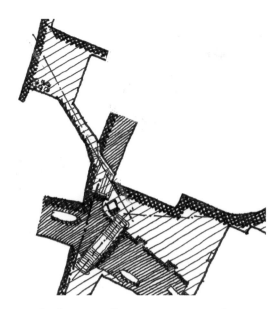

3.8 The dry Campiello Mosca contrasts with quaylike Campo San Pantalon.

Activity

Modern-day planning for urban open spaces emphasizes the need for a programming of activities to appropriately enliven a square, and indeed, activities are the main reason for dealing with squares in the first place. Where suitable, accommodation for activities such as cafés, markets, spontaneous play, theatrical or musical events, and the needs of elders should be a primary focus of the design of urban public spaces, giving identity, goal, interest, and purpose. This may appear obvious, but many a dead square demonstrates a failure to adequately plan for such activities. Most of the campi clearly serve a combination of such purposes well. It may seem that there are exceptions, such as ceremonial forecourts or quiet places of calm and repose, but these are themselves activities, meriting careful accommodation if and when appropriate to the nature of the square in its urban context. Examples of the latter include Campo Santa Maria Nova, and some of the campielli, such as Mosca.

A special case on the subject of activity is public assembly, not so much for theatrical or musical events but as a manifestation of civic demonstration, whether in celebration, support, or protest. Iconic public spaces on a very large scale depend on large cities to support their viability and to avoid an everyday sense of lifeless emptiness. Piazza San Marco is the Venetian equivalent, although rather modest in size compared to some over-scaled civic plazas, old and new alike. Squares on the scale of the campi are of a different faith and order, arising from an urban way of life long fostered in the Old World but to a lesser degree in the New.

Amenity

The vibrant manifestation of such activity depends on more than demand and intent. Elements of amenity, whether large and permanent or smaller and more temporary, play a crucial part. Trees are significant amenities in many of the campi, but in insular groupings. While many American squares are actually leafy parks, pavements dominate here—sometimes with no trees at all. Other factors can support a vibrant space, as at Campo San Stefano, and they can also fall short, as at Campo dei Frari. Permanent freestanding elements, including towers, flagpoles, kiosks, wellheads, and sculptural monuments, play a large part in enlivening the campi, along with wall-mounted features such as awnings and balconies. And while water—along with embankments, steps, and bridges in the Venetian context—enhances a number of campi, it is not necessarily a compelling aspect of a successful square: while Campi San Pantalon, San Barnaba, San Zanipolo, Santa Maria Nova, and the Piazzetta feature water, Campi San Giacomo, San Polo, Santa Margherita, San Stefano, and Piazza San Marco do not (Fig. 3.8).

Furniture

"Furniture" refers here to elements of amenity that a square may feature which are not directly engaged with its sidewalls and are, generally, movable. Such elements can screen or sequence the experience of a square and may also be central to the facilitation of activity. Benches, various types of structured shade, and temporary structures such as stages, kiosks, and food booths all play a part (Fig. 3.9). The grouping of these three-dimensional elements so as to articulate the space of the square—not to defuse and obscure it—is normally the goal. Zones of unobstructed, flexible open space should be a result of the defining impacts of such elements, in conjunction with the sidewall configurations themselves. (In this unique context, another element of furniture in most of the campi would be the assorted canal watercraft.) Observation indicates that seating should, perhaps surprisingly, be generally located directly alongside pedestrian routes, rather than secluded from them, as seen in Campi San Giacomo, San Polo, Santa Margherita, San Zanipolo, and Santa Maria Nova, not to mention Piazza San Marco and the Piazzetta.

3.9 The mixup of benches and market stalls in Campo Santa Margherita.

Scale

In a lesson that is seemingly self-evident but often overlooked, spaces should be scaled to their levels of physical and visual activity: Campo San Rocco seems too small; Campi San Polo and Santa Maria Formosa can seem too large. Campo San Barnaba seems "just about right" (Fig. 3.10). Alexander, concluding that modern-day public squares tend to be too large, posits an optimum diameter of 60 feet, which is consistent with many of these campi and the sub-areas of the larger ones.[16] Lynch in turn states that spatial width dimensions of around 25 meters (82 feet) are immediately comfortable and well-dimensioned in a social context, and also asserts that dimensions greater than 110 meters (360 feet) are seldom found in good city spaces.[17] Well-known American squares often reach or exceed these larger dimensions.

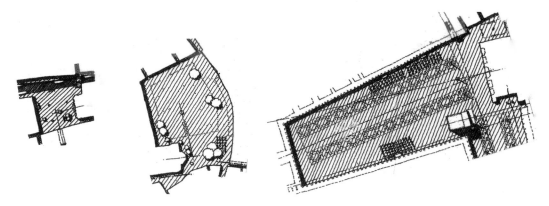

3.10 Campo San Barnaba is about 100 feet on a side, while Campo San Polo is twice that. Piazza San Marco at roughly 600 feet in its long dimension significantly exceeds Lynch's postulate and might not work very well as an urban square were it not for its unique combination of qualities, plus, of course, its fame.

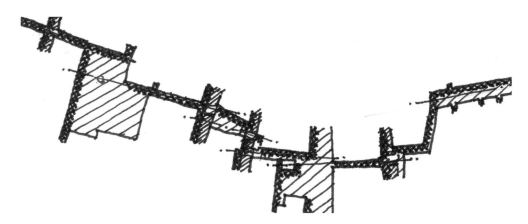

3.11 Part of the Campo San Stefano/Piazza San Marco linking sequence.

Sequence

Most successful urban open spaces exist in a dynamic ensemble of sequence and connectivity. An informed crafting of sequence is key to fostering a desirable variation of experience in time, featuring intrigue and surprise, repose and activity, intimacy and expansiveness. Several Venetian sequences (Pantalon–Barnaba, Stefano–Marco, Zanipolo–Nova) have demonstrated this by connecting a variety of squares, themselves having varied and differing sets of qualities, with relatively short, contrasting linking passages (Fig. 3.11).

Spatial Variegation

The campi present a specific array of strategies to vary, anchor, or focus each space. Freestanding or projecting elements—often churches in these cases—can help define and elaborate the space, as at Campi San Giacomo, San Polo, Santa Margherita, and Santa Maria Formosa. Tree groups can also serve this purpose, acting in contrast with open areas, with ground-plane landscaping being reserved to limited areas of appropriate impact. These are the case at Campi San Giacomo,

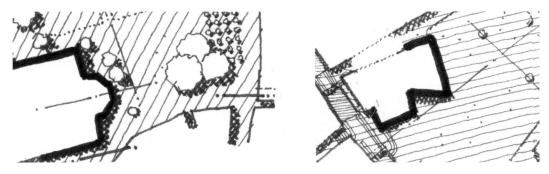

3.12 A projecting element in San Polo; a freestanding element in Sant'Angelo.

3.13 A tower in Santa Maria Formosa; "theatrical" spatial definition at Santa Maria Nova; obtuse- and acute-angled sidewall relationships at San Giacomo.

San Polo, Santa Margherita, and Santa Maria Nova. And the campi demonstrate that "foreground" elements, which can provide a sense of focus for the space, are especially effective when located off-center, angled and/or engaged with "background" sidewalls. This treatment is seen at many of the campi as well as Piazza San Marco (Fig. 3.12).

A special version of such an off-center foreground element, anchoring the ensemble of space and form, arises from the many churches associated with the campi: their bell towers. These are often engaged with the sidewall fabric, as at Campi San Giacomo, dei Frari, and Santa Maria Formosa, or may be freestanding, as at Piazza San Marco. In addition to bell towers, tower-like elements of civic, commercial, or residential structures also proliferate in the Old World as anchors

for urban squares. Spatial configurations that recall a theatrical audience/stage spatial duality, both to celebrate "urban life as theater" and to facilitate actual use as a performance venue, can enliven what might otherwise be a more mundane urban space, as at Campi San Polo, Sant'Angelo, and Santa Maria Nova. And while rectilinear footprints for squares can work well if particularized by special conditions, gently obtuse and acute sidewall angular relationships at adjoining or facing sidewalls, as well as convex and concave conditions, are of great value in terms of contributing to a sense that the square is a living, evolving part of the larger urban experience. This is the rule rather than the exception among the campi, as at Campi San Giacomo, San Stefano, and Sant'Angelo, as well as Piazza San Marco and the Piazzetta (Fig. 3.13).

Sidewall Variegation

As noted above in "Sidewalls" and elsewhere, effective sidewalls involve a number of strategies working together to achieve variegation (Fig. 3.14):

- A close range of surface texture and color, with occasional well-placed contrasting accents.
- A number of fenestration schemes, the result being neither too regularized nor too variegated.
- A variety of ground floor treatments: degrees of openness, sill heights, canopy types, signage.
- Visual interest which embodies "fractal scalability."
- A lack of overall façade symmetry, in favor of zones of localized symmetry.

- A strong, nearly contiguous sidewall, with variety provided by atypical roofscapes, balconies, eave heights, window types, and skyline elements such as towers, rooftop balconies, chimneys and cupolas.

Proportion

As noted above in "The Campi as a Matrix of Spatial Types," attention to proportion in the spatial footprint is key to the nature and effectiveness of squares. Simple square or rectangular footprints can achieve a "sense of place" if particularized by special conditions, as at Campi San Barnaba and Santa Maria Nova. In contrast, where appropriate, attenuated triangular footprints impart a

dynamic quality that fosters movement, as at Campi San Pantalon and Santa Margherita. But further attenuation, with the sidewalls again parallel, represents a transition to a street space, as at Rio Terà Canal: different in nature from an urban square (Fig. 3.15).

Regarding spatial width in proportion to sidewall height, a dimensional ratio of width to height that is neither too constrained (more a street than a square) nor too broad (losing definition and focus) seems optimum for an effective urban space. In the case of the campi, a rough 3:1 ratio is consistently found, while other research suggests a maximum ratio of 6:1 to achieve a satisfactory level of enclosure.[18]

3.14 A sidewall of Campo San Stefano, indicating localized symmetries and other aspects of variegation.

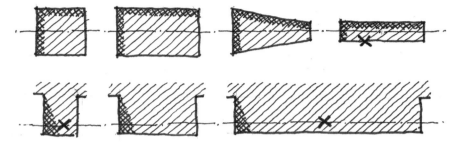

3.15 Sequential diagrams of spatial and height proportion.

3.16 A range of spatial definition varying from more enclosed to more open, at Santa Maria Nova, Santa Maria Formosa, San Barnaba, and San Pantalon.

Spatial Definition

Last but not least, the degree of a sense of enclosure is an important variable among the campi. Here there are no good or bad cases, but a sort of continuum ranging from a high degree of enclosure to a significant sense of openness along one face. Any more opening up than this and a site would arguably become too wide-open to be perceived as an urban square. A high degree of enclosure characterizes the smallest, Campo Santa Maria Nova, and the largest, Piazza San Marco. While a large number of campi are also highly defined, convexities or corners mean the whole space can't be seen at once, as at Campi San Giacomo and Santa Maria Formosa. In another common way that enclosure prevails but with definition somewhat reduced, a canal along one side opens up two adjacent corners, as at Campi San Barnaba and San Zanipolo. Finally, one side is more wide-open to adjacency, rendering the campo an alcove of space, as at Campi San Pantalon and San Vidal (Fig. 3.16). (At the Piazzetta that prospect becomes virtually unbounded. Open at both ends, the space can seem more a place to pass through than a place to spend time in.) The campielli reward study as exemplars of the alcove case, while a few, such as Campiello Mosca, retain a sense of full enclosure.

• • •

In summary, these Venetian squares, without the barriers, breaches, and noise of trafficways and parking, and without the particularizing issues of topography—

- but with use by people as pedestrians paramount, whether individually or in groups,
- with the benefit of a unique urban morphology which distances them, as objects for study, from the distracting panoply of formal approaches to urban space,
- and with abundant evidence that they help foster an enviable way of life—offer a rich variety of specific lessons in the crafting of effective urban space.

One could posit that it's too big a stretch to look for such lessons from these urban spaces, in a city that had its heyday in the 15th century, to productively apply in the quite different culture and setting of modern times. But one could also offer that human nature hasn't actually changed that dramatically since those days, and that a corresponding examination of modern-day squares ought to reveal some productive and interesting connections.

4 America's Urban Spaces

How well could these findings about some unique old-world squares help to assess, improve, and design modern-day urban spaces? To address that question, some general observations about today's squares are called for, and although a book could be written about that subject, some basic aspects hold true. In terms of the 20th and 21st centuries in the USA, most places that are called town squares are actually town parks. In the headlong development of the country, new towns and settlements were customarily laid out—platted—in one or another version of an orthogonal grid, and the most common town square was a courthouse square: a block in the middle of town, with the county courthouse in the middle of the block (Fig. 4.1). The building's surrounding grounds feature lawns, plantings, trees, pathways, and benches. Some towns that are not county seats also feature such a

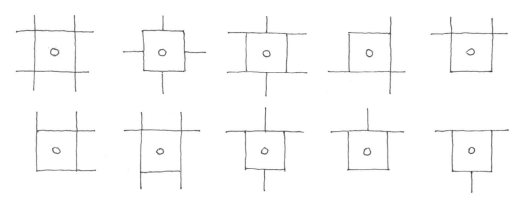

4.1 The variety of county courthouse square plan types found in Tennessee. The first and second are the most typical types throughout the country.[19]

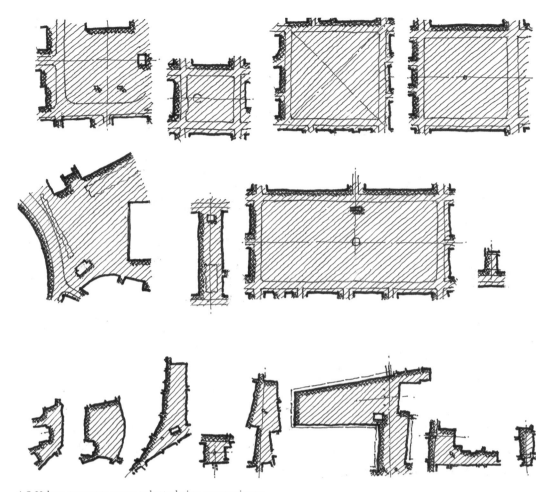

4.2 Urban squares: some selected size comparisons.
Top: Nashville Public Square; Pioneer Courthouse Square, Portland; Rittenhouse Square, Philadelphia; Jackson Square, New Orleans.
Middle: City Hall Plaza, Boston; Market Square, Knoxville; Washington Square Park, NYC; Paley Park, NYC.
Bottom: The Venetian Campi.

central park space, sometimes called a village green, often focusing on a gazebo, bandstand, or monument. The point for these purposes is that the town square as a park (a somewhat residual perimeter park in the case of the county seats) became widely established as what was meant by urban open space in America, in contrast to the paved plazas and market squares of Europe. They are more in the nature of places of respite than foci for urban life, particularly in an age when urban life is still being rediscovered as a desirable condition.

Many so-called squares in large cities are also predominantly green parks, such as Rittenhouse Square in Philadelphia,

Jackson Square in New Orleans, or Manhattan's Washington Square Park (Fig. 4.2). Rittenhouse is 500 feet square, and a cursory search of well-regarded town squares in the USA, such as Decatur Square in Georgia, Healdsburg Plaza in California, or the squares of Savannah, Georgia—all actually parks—finds them typically ranging from 250 to 300 feet square and more: in excess of the scale of the Venetian squares, and of Alexander's or Lynch's recommendations as well.

That said, what of urban squares in the USA that are largely paved, as opposed to being urban parks? They do exist, but typically as anomalies rather than time-honored types: exceptions,

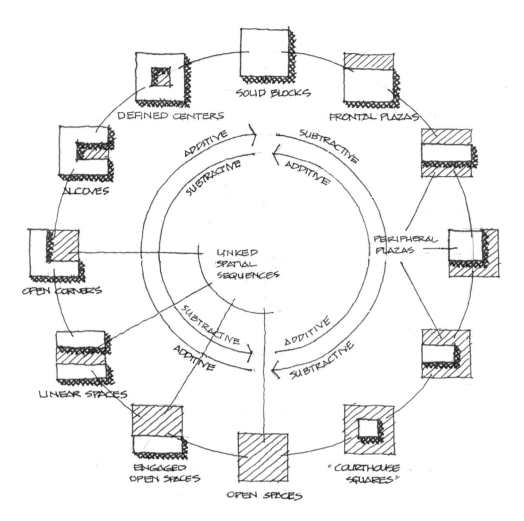

4.3 A circle of urban open space types.
The narratives that follow begin at the top with "Solid Blocks" and proceed clockwise, ending at "Defined Centers."

rather than the rule. Portland, Oregon's Pioneer Courthouse Square, built in 1984, emulates the above precedent of setting aside a central block in a gridded city as a town square. But despite the relatively small size of Portland's blocks, this brick-paved square is still over 200 feet on a side, not counting the space occupied by the surrounding streets. This renders it a bit more of a void than a place, despite significant amenity design efforts on its perimeters and the mid-to-tall building profiles surrounding.

These two archetypes can be visualized as taking their places on a transformational sequence of such types, ranging from the "open" block exemplified by Portland's square—and its green relative, the courthouse square or park—to the opposite pole of a "solid" block of American townscape fabric. The intervening stages between these poles comprise further archetypes—the anomalies—of the several versions of defined urban open space that crop up across the country. The sequence can be visualized either as additive, with the empty block gradually filled in, or subtractive, with the solid block subject to sequentially larger removals (Fig. 4.3). Each such anomaly in turn represents its own set of spatial variations, and each merits its own discussion.[20]

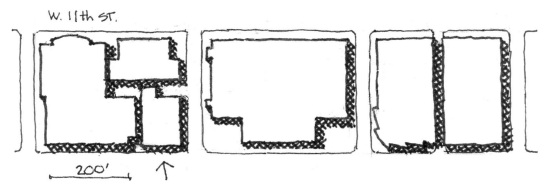

4.4 An example of three adjoining blocks in downtown Kansas City, MO:
Left: central void; middle: solid block; right: centerline alley.
Note: in the ground plans that follow, scale varies from type to type, but plans grouped on a page are to the same scale. Direction of north varies.

Solid Blocks

The base case of an urban plaza is its absence, and this is the nature of many towns in the US. Built-up blocks, whether square or rectangular (or irregular in footprint, as can be the case in the older towns of the Northeast) are seldom truly solid and filled up with built construction, unless a single large building does indeed fill up the block. They generally have either alleyways or central voids for service access (Fig. 4.4). (Service needs as well as security aspects render these sometimes interesting "internal open spaces" a challenge for ideas of repurposing them for public use.) In smaller cities and towns, the back halves of blocks flanking the main street often end up being parking lots. Demolitions, resulting in vacant lots, constitute further exceptions to the solidity of the block, as some of the following types will reveal.

Frontal and Peripheral Plazas

Windswept and largely empty plazas, such as that fronting New York City's Seagram Building, were primarily efforts to pump up the importance of the building rather than to provide space designed for activities. While in such cases the open space directly engages a sidewall, the rest of the perimeter remains open to surrounding streets. Worse, object buildings will often pull back from two or even three exposures, as if they were a sculpture on a podium, the residual open space that remains having even less of a sense of place. Two other cases of frontal plazas, among many, illustrate the benefit of *furniture*—kiosk-like outbuildings in these cases—as well as the *amenity* of significant tree groupings, to help populate and define frontal plazas that would otherwise be rather too similar to Seagram's (Fig. 4.5). (Such italics will signify features that accord—or don't—with the findings from the Venetian squares.)

Courthouse Squares

With frontal plazas extending on all sides, here rendered in landscaped lawns that surround a county courthouse, this ubiquitous type finds its place in the sequence (Fig. 4.6). In the case of such central buildings, *diagonal* routes are notably obstructed. Both this type and the next are characterized by one degree or another of openness, their nature typically being far removed from

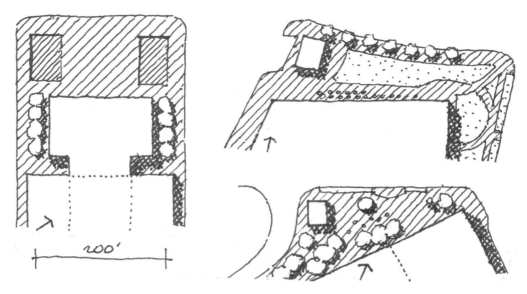

4.5 Ground plans of frontal plazas.
Seagram Plaza; Strawberry Park, Merrifield, VA; US Bank Plaza, Cleveland.

the room-like quality of the campi. These prototypical American squares are ultimately delimited by urban sidewalls flanking the surrounding streets. As the square is approached along these streets its presence is gradually revealed, in contrast to the tightly focused or *obscured* entry experiences of the Venetian campi.

"Open Spaces"

The term refers to urban spaces that aren't immediately bounded by sidewalls (Fig. 4.7). Revisiting Portland's Pioneer Courthouse Square, it's an example of this type, being one of relatively few American paved plazas that comprise a whole block. Morphologically, it's the opposite number to the "solid block." The Portland square accommodates a variety of *furniture, amenities,* and *activities,* but is primarily a large, flat, brick pavement (which, to be sure, facilitates desirable pedestrian circulation on the diagonal), that is isolated from amenities in adjoining buildings by the surrounding streetscape (Fig. 4.8).

Some other large urban open spaces aren't quite as isolated, by virtue of having some direct adjacencies to boundary buildings on one or more sides, but the issue of isolation remains. In the case of Boston's City Hall Plaza the perimeter is porous and ill-defined, in contrast to its supposed inspiration, Siena's Piazza di

4.6 Maury County Courthouse Square, Columbia, TN: View to north. Photo by Marian Moffett.

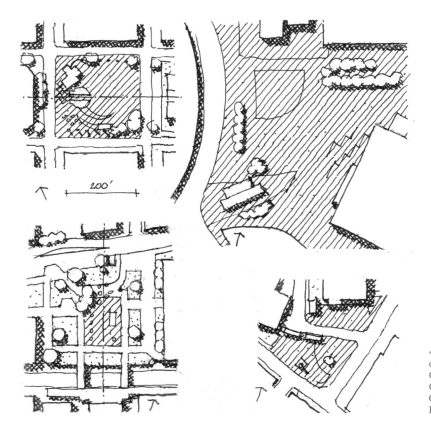

4.7 Ground plans of open spaces. Clockwise: Pioneer Courthouse Square; City Hall Plaza; Parade Plaza; El Presidio Plaza.

Campo (or to Venice's campi). At New London, Connecticut's Parade Plaza, a somewhat similar profile exists, albeit smaller and cut in two by a transverse street and likewise defined by spaced-apart buildings. Neither plaza features adequate *amenity* to enliven it, excepting the self-enlivening occurrences of infrequent mass attendance events.

The central rectangular pavement of Tucson's El Presidio Plaza is relatively intimate in scale, but a complex array of walks and planted areas extending from all sides diminish that impression while resulting in considerable separations from adjacent buildings. Streets to the north and south further isolate the plaza, abetted by a tall retaining wall condition on the south. Plant materials, small shade structures, a fountain, and some sculptural pieces enliven the ensemble, but its isolation and somewhat chaotic layout augur against a memorable image for the plaza, or a sense of integration in its urban context.

Engaged Open Spaces

While some of the above cases feature directly adjoining boundary buildings, none of them quite read as full-width engaged backdrops for the adjacent squares. This latter case is the opposite number to the frontal plaza, with the building now secondary to a deeper, more significant open space that it engages (Fig. 4.9). In this first step in an additive sequence of types, plazas remain isolated by streets on the other sides. The degree to which these open exposures are mitigated often constitutes their success as attractive places for people.

Constrained entry approaches serve well to *obscure* the view in at Key West's Mallory Square, its long seaboard frontage

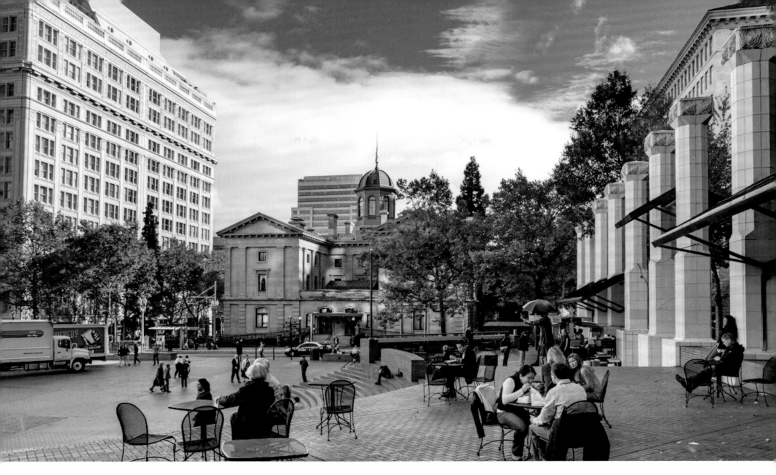

4.8 Pioneer Courthouse Square, Portland, OR: View to east.
Note the wide range of building scale at the perimeter. While some conditions around the edge are attractive for use by individuals or small groups, they directly adjoin the surrounding streets in many cases. The main open space, too large for such uses, is scaled for market or mass-attendance events, and can seem vacant at other times. Photo by Alamy.

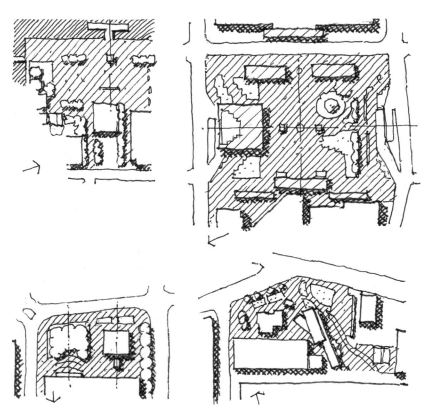

4.9 Ground plans of engaged open spaces. Clockwise: Mallory Square; Civic Plaza; Larkin Square; Miller Plaza.

(the Gulf taking the place of bounding streetscapes in this case) vaguely recalling that of the Piazzetta. Two elongated pedestrianways, flanked by and overhung with greenery, fully isolate the experience of the square from their streetscape entry points. Its large size is most effective during crowded sunset observances.

As with all these urban space types, *scale* varies greatly. Albuquerque's 400-foot-square Civic Plaza, directly engaged on one side by civic buildings and pergolas, is arguably too open and undefined to serve as an inviting destination for individuals or small groups, despite efforts at *amenity*. Chattanooga's Miller Plaza and Buffalo's Larkin Square have the initial advantage of manageable scale, and they make notable use of *intervening elements*. At Chattanooga, a pavilion building so dominates the ensemble that a well-defined pedestrian open space is lacking,

4.10 Larkin Square, Buffalo, NY: View to southeast. With dignified turn-of-the-century buildings and a parking garage beyond as backdrops, this large, irregular space was developed as a food truck and entertainment venue, featuring a variety of open pavilions, a renovated gas station, varied pavements, lawns, trees, and tennis courts. The result, though still sort of wide-open, is a variety of subtly defined and linked spaces. Photo courtesy of Larkin Square.

Linear Spaces

Urban spaces in this country that begin to do a good job of fostering urban life at a human scale often turn out to be pedestrianized streets. These "linear spaces" (let's say they exceed twice their width in length) could be thought of as the next additive step in this progression of urban spatial types, as if the engaged open space were mirrored to become bound on flanking sides. (Alternatively, the next step could be one of turning a corner with the engaged boundary resulting in an "open corner," a type which follows. The two types are, in fact, co-equals in this progression.)

Blocks-long streetscape "malls" are a big step up from car-focused streets, as at Charlottesville, Virginia, or Cape May, New Jersey, though their linear continuity and *proportion* inevitably mean they are still more like streets than places (Fig. 4.11).[21] An end terminated by a building, as at Burlington, Vermont's Church Street, affords an added measure of containment. In a few cases, significant gaps in the streetwall, or a less-than-straight profile for the pedway (both found at "Last Chance Gulch" in Helena, Montana), likewise vary the spatial experience. Despite these variables, urban

the overall square seeming a series of separate experiences. Larkin Square is also open to the streetscape on much of its periphery, but views in are serially *obscured* by a playful variety of kiosks and shade structures, arrayed in an artfully skewed composition (Fig. 4.10). And while they subdivide the square's paved portion into semi-separate enclaves, a sense of the overall composition is still perceived.

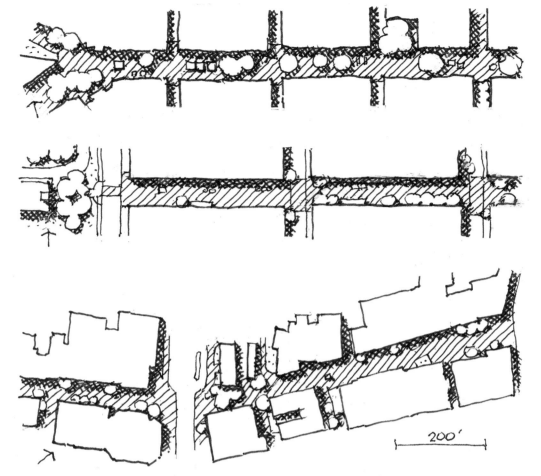

4.11 Ground Plans of long linear spaces.
Main Street, Charlottesville, VA, of eight blocks;
Church Street, Burlington, VT, of four blocks; Last
Chance Gulch, Helena, MT, of three blocks.

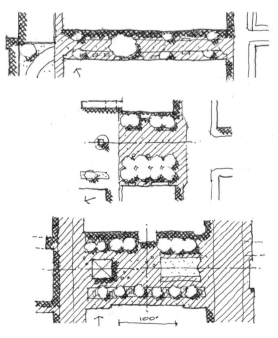

4.12 Ground Plans of short linear spaces.
Brightleaf Square; Centerway Square; Rockville
Town Square.

streetscapes are not urban spaces in the normal sense, but they can nonetheless incorporate desirable features, including *activity, amenity, sidewall variegation,* and, of course, isolation from vehicular traffic.

When urban conditions limit the pedestrian street to one block in length, more of a sense of place can begin to emerge (Fig. 4.12). Durham, North Carolina's Brightleaf Square, while still street-like in its proportions, is visually terminated at both ends. Corning, New York's Centerway Square stands out for its squarish proportions at 100 by 80 feet, but is open to bypassing streets and long axes beyond, increasing its perceived length and diminishing its sense of place. Rockville Town Square in Maryland is larger at 120 by 200 feet, but is also bounded at the ends, and features a well-scaled central

4.13 Rockville Town Square, Rockville, MD: View to west.
Many significant features are visible: fenced outdoor dining, a kiosk, central open space and a fountain, lawn, flanking tree rows, simply variegated pavement, and closure at the ends by street sidewalls beyond. The space's qualities of enclosure and symmetry imposes a desirable sense of calm respite. Larkin Square, by contrast, employs idiosyncratic and angular relationships appropriate to a youthful and energetic vibe. Photo courtesy of Dan Reed.

space flanked by *elements* and *amenities,* including a pavilion, a lawn, an enfilade of outdoor dining, and fully engaged, permeable, and interesting *sidewalls.* As a further nicety, paver treatments extend into the flanking curbless streets (Fig. 4.13).

A special case of "linear" spaces, distinct from pedestrianized streets or street-like urban spaces, is the vacant lot, a ubiquitous feature in towns of a certain size that have a several-blocks-long main street in the center of town (Fig. 4.14). The cases in question involve improvements to the lot that once contained a building. All too often such improvements are cursory, due to a lack of funds or will in the community, perhaps consisting of picnic tables, rudimentary pavements, and minimal landscape materials. And, as

the sidewalls likely were never intended to be exposed to view, rough masonry is the norm. However, better pavements, trees, and permanent shade structures have turned many vacant lots into inviting adjuncts to the street, shop, restaurant, or bar. Sometimes there are alleys leading from the street to the back of the block (frequently to a parking lot) that have been improved as respite areas, and which benefit from sidewalls that were always exposed and thus have existing doors and windows in keeping with those on the street exposure. New construction can be another variable, when it serves to define adjoining urban spaces where no such space existed previously.

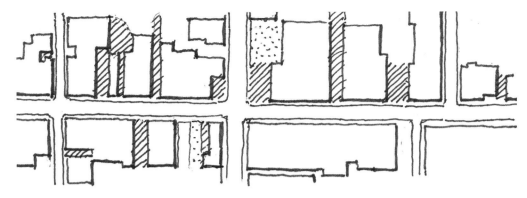

4.14 Ten redeveloped vacant lots and alleys are to be found along Sumter, SC's Main Street. Its central crossroads even features flanking open corner spaces (resulting in a rather weakened overall spatial quality), that being the next type in this progression.relationships at San Giacomo.

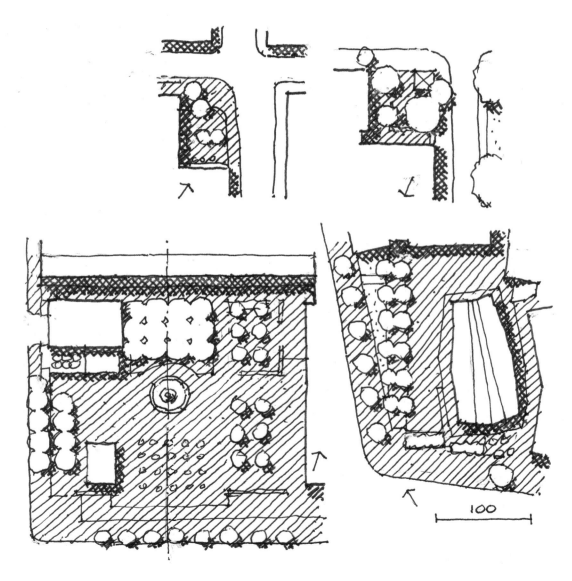

100

4.15 Ground Plans of open corner spaces.
Clockwise: Parkersburg, WV; Princeton, NJ; Silver Spring, MD; Cincinnati, OH.

4.16 Courtyard Adjoining Palmer Square, Princeton, NJ: View to south.
In this view from the sidewalk, a corner kiosk effectively defines a space that would otherwise be an open corner. Quality pavements, seating, and plant materials, the norm in this privileged setting, undeniably contribute to the appeal of the space. That said, more economical such choices would not necessarily mean a less engaging result. Photo courtesy of Palmer Square.

Open Corners

Open corners are found pretty much everywhere, and at widely varying scales (Fig. 4.15). They're often part of a single building development wherein a corner has been carved out to accommodate a sometimes rather pointless entry plaza. Birmingham, Sacramento, Peoria, Des Moines, Dodge City, Danville, Rapid City—every city has them. Their primary drawback as urban spaces is the way that spatial definition, begun at the inboard corner, leaks out into the street and beyond on the outboard corner. Visual exposure is, to be sure, often the mission of these open corners, but sometimes this is achieved at the price of their ending up as uninviting places for pedestrians to spend time.

The Blue Cross building's plaza in Parkersburg, West Virginia is typical of many open corner plazas that have minimal outboard containment, and its random table and chair seating is perfunctory and rather uninviting, which is also typical. A similarly scaled plaza adjoining Palmer Square in Princeton, New Jersey, benefits from the often-missing *amenity* of mature trees, and the *furniture* of a kiosk in its outboard corner does a good deal to help define a sense of place and separation (Fig. 4.16).

At a larger scale, Veterans Plaza in Silver Spring, Maryland benefits from skillful contemporary design, including a sleek skating shelter. Being located inboard, the shelter doesn't help as much with definition, but a banked lawn with trees assumes that role with some success.

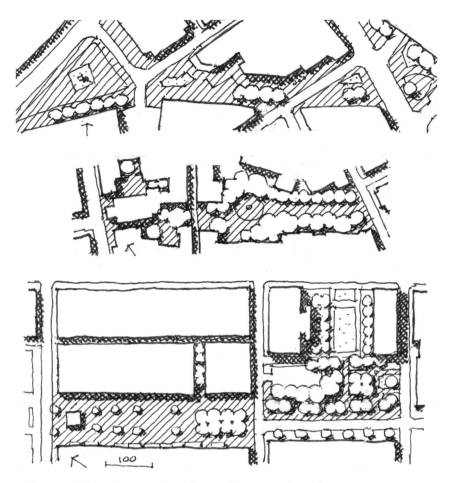

4.17 Ground plans of square-like and street-like spaces linked in sequence. Portland, ME; Boston, MA; Knoxville, TN.

The shelter does define an adjoining linear space alongside a commercial frontage, adding complexity and *sequence* to the overall experience. Cincinnati's Fountain Square expands the *scale* of its open corner past the limits for retaining a sense of place, such that the space devolves to a grid of smaller sections. A centerpiece fountain is somewhat overwhelmed by the overall scale. A significant kiosk building adjoining an outboard corner, plus a temporary stage at the open corner, provide partial *spatial variegation* and containment. A level change at the perimeter means the presence of monumental steps, subtly isolating the square from the life of the sidewalk. Developed as an event venue, the square does address the importance of programmed *activity* to the life of an urban space.

Linked Spatial Sequences

Towns and cities may feature several of our open space types, typically located rather randomly with respect to each other. But occasionally a linked *sequence,* either as paired with a "preparatory" space, as are some of the campi, or in combination with a linked *series* of such spaces, affords an enhanced experience, each leading to and contrasting with the next. Sequences of squares alternating with street-like spaces afford *proportional* variety (Fig. 4.17). Portland, Maine's Congress and Temple Streets are linked by a sequence of four such spaces that benefit from angled relationships to flanking buildings,

4.18 Market Square, Knoxville, TN: View to south.
Its paved open space is tempered by a grove of mature trees, leading to a small, shady urban park beyond. Modest late 19th-century commercial sidewalls flank the elongated rectangle of space, which originally centered on an 1897 market house, since demolished. Sizing the main body of the resulting open space for use as a wintertime skating rink has resulted in an overlarge empty quarter at the focus of the square, excepting at farmers market days.

resulting in a dynamic spatial experience that helps ameliorate their large scale. At Boston's Old North Church, the intimate scale of its churchyards contrasts with the linear "mall" beyond, all softened by tree cover and their irregular boundaries of old urban fabric. And Knoxville, Tennessee's Market Square has the proportion of a very wide street, linked to a small urban park to the south and, in turn, an activities lawn developed in an adjoining vacant lot that links to the street (Fig. 4.18).

Four further selected cases develop spatial sequences within more closely defined areas (Fig. 4.19). Baltimore's Market Place flanks its main "alcove" of space with many *activities,* including a food court gallery, nightspots, and a children's museum, and is linked to an events lawn. A variety of seating and a freestanding pavilion enliven and articulate the space. In Portland, Oregon, the PSU Urban Center development effectively contain the flanks of an engaged open space, the irregular building boundaries accommodating the novelty of a through-passing trolley track while delineating a *sequenced entry*. And Old Town Square in Fort Collins, Colorado mixes new and old urban fabric and links with adjoining spaces to form a complex

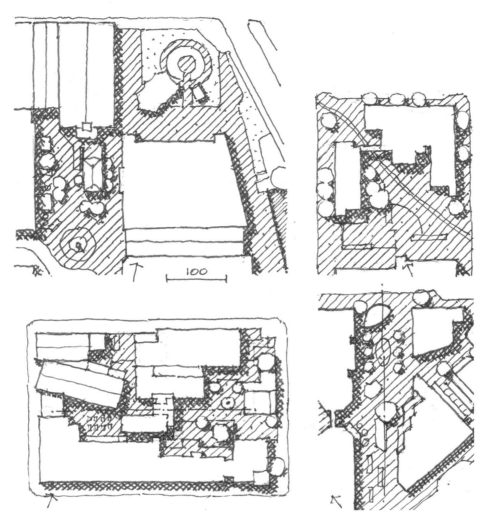

4.19 Ground plans of sequentially linked square-like spaces.
Clockwise: Baltimore, MD; Portland, OR; Fort Collins, CO; San Francisco, CA.

and intriguingly angular spatial array. An events stage, water features, tree cover, and extensive outdoor seating and dining opportunities complement the definition, variety, and scale of its spaces.

San Francisco's Ghirardelli Square, considered the first successful adaptive reuse project in the country, is also one of its most successful examples of linked urban open spaces (Fig. 4.20). Dating from 1964 as a mixed-use attraction with restaurant, retail, and office tenants, this ensemble of buildings and courtyards is especially notable among American urban spaces for a number of aspects, many of which recall corresponding aspects of the Venetian campi:

- Its closely ordered sequence of courtyards, all irregular in footprint.
- Subsidiary spaces that step down to lower entries on its sloping site, taking full advantage of the grade change to craft the ascent or descent into sequential experiences of their own.
- Shifts in the sequential layout of the main open spaces with pinch points between them, such that only partial views beyond to the next space are visible.
- Whether older or newer, buildings and pavements that consistently employ the single material of red brick, a welcome foil to the development's highly varied configurations and details.

4.20 Ghirardelli Square: View to southwest.
One of the most notable examples in the US of urban squares arrayed in a sequence, the development incorporates both historic and modern building fabric, and navigates substantial changes in topography. Photo courtesy of Jamestown Urban Management.

- The original chocolate factory building forming a backdrop for the ensemble, sharing with other perimeter buildings a role of partially isolating the sequence of open spaces from urban exposures beyond.
- A seamless assemblage of buildings from the early 1900s and modern-era structures, the latter making no effort to appear historicist yet being sensitively proportioned and detailed for a harmonious whole.
- Substantial trees, serving as focus elements as opposed to setting a park-like theme.
- A scheme of simple and understated but festive night lighting.

- An approach notable for the interposition of projecting and freestanding elements, such as gazebos and stairwell structures, to articulate the spaces.
- Understated graphics, including the boldly scaled but tastefully designed skyline signage.

Alcoves

"Alcoves" of space, a mode of spatial definition among the campi, are found over a wide variety of scales and uses in the US (Fig. 4.21). Such spaces are typically dead-ended recesses in an urban streetwall, as contrasted with the open-ended nature of street-like spaces, and they represent the most well-defined and contained urban open spaces discussed so far. New Orleans' Piazza d'Italia, Charles Moore's flamboyant homage to Italy and a case of *spatial variegation*, has yet to be fully enclosed by urban fabric as was hoped, thus rendering it an alcove. At Lincoln, Nebraska's pleasantly sequestered Haymarket Square Courtyard, an entrance gate and initial neck of space effectively *obscure* its full extent on approach; the alleyway beyond could potentially afford further such development. This courtyard's scale, and that of New York City's well-known Paley Park, are similar

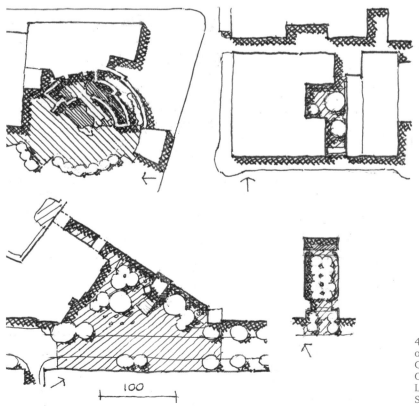

4.21 Ground Plans of alcove spaces. Clockwise: New Orleans, LA; Lincoln, NE; NYC; Silver Spring, MD.

100

4.22 Silver Plaza, Silver Springs, MD: View to north.
Lively and varied sidewall treatments bound the space and the through-passing street. Tower, staircase, and ground plane elements further vary the experience of the relatively modest plaza. Its "right triangle" of space affords unexpected and dynamic views in and out: in contrast to a more conventionally rectangular footprint, it either funnels toward the narrow walkway at its inner corner or expands toward the street. Photo from Google Maps.

to that of some of the campielli. At Silver Plaza in Silver Spring, Maryland, a retail development employs *spatial variegation* in defining a triangular plaza (Fig. 4.22). It faces a narrow through-passing street, which is incorporated in the life of the plaza during open-air markets. On approach from the street, the opening-up of the plaza is effectively *obscured* almost until it is reached. Intervening *freestanding elements* subdivide, populate, and enliven the space.

Sundance Square in Fort Worth is unusual among urban squares in the US, benefiting from direct sidewall adjacencies on three sides as well as wooded buffers along the fourth (Fig. 4.23). Plus, the north-south central axis of Main Street is closed to traffic, doubling the size of the contiguous pedestrian precinct. The square has much to recommend it, but its size augurs against a well-defined sense of place, despite its many *amenities*: morphologically it's an alcove, but too large to read as one. At the other extreme in scale, modest but often well-accoutered alcoves that afford alfresco space for bars and cafés are ubiquitous across the country. In Rapid City, South Dakota, a wide alcove accommodates two bars side by side. Bozeman, Montana's bar and café patios sport several spatial types, including alcoves that face a side street or an alley. In such cases, alcoves afford a street exposure while providing a sense of place and containment, and also improving aspects of control and security.

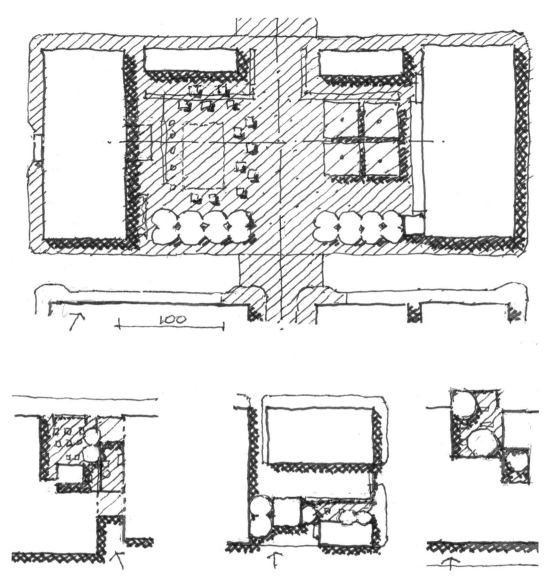

4.23 Ground plans of alcove spaces, among the largest and smallest of the type.
Sundance Square, Fort Worth, TX; Café-Bar Alcoves in Rapid City, SD and Bozeman, MT.

Defined Centers

A final urban spatial type completes the *spatial definition* of an urban place with building fabric, isolating it from nearby streets. The precedent of the lightwell in the middle of a dense urban residential block comes to mind, but those are typically narrow, tall, and insular. For such a space to participate in the life of the city, gaps in the perimeter must exist as entries to the otherwise highly contained space. The best versions of the type, enclosed and room-like, embody the attributes exemplified by many of the campi (Fig. 4.24). Some such cases approach this level of definition by assembling several buildings in close proximity around a central space, as at Phoenix's "Patriots Park." The centerpiece of a downtown development, it's actually a linked spatial sequence, bridging over to a raised extension on the adjoining

102

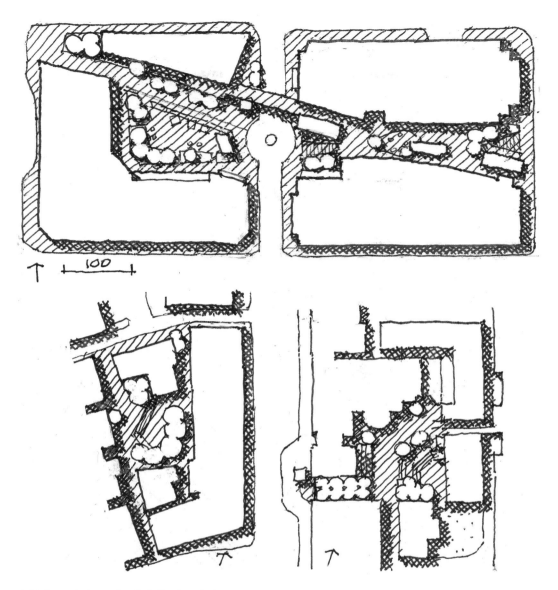

4.24 Ground plans of well-defined central spaces.
Above: Patriots Park, Phoenix, AZ. Below: Bicentennial and Eagle Squares, Concord, NH.

block. *Amenities* of fountains, trees, shade structures, and a *variegated periphery* create a contemporary urban oasis. At a more domestic scale, two different blocks in Concord, New Hampshire, each define central spaces with a combination of new and old urban fabric. Their levels step down in response to topography and help *variegate* the space, as do their irregular *sidewall* configurations.

San Francisco's adjoining Cannery and Anchorage Square projects exhibit a more complete embodiment of full enclosure (Figs. 4.25, 4.26). Each full-block development defines a central courtyard, while offset passages to the periphery permit the public to flow through. (Also of note, a substantial linear open space adjoins the Cannery.) More intimately scaled versions of the type proliferate in Santa Fe, New Mexico, as at the Georgia O'Keeffe Museum, where the gated entry to its central courtyard both welcomes entry and partially *obscures* the view in. Nearby, a one-story commercial building incorporates fully five courtyards

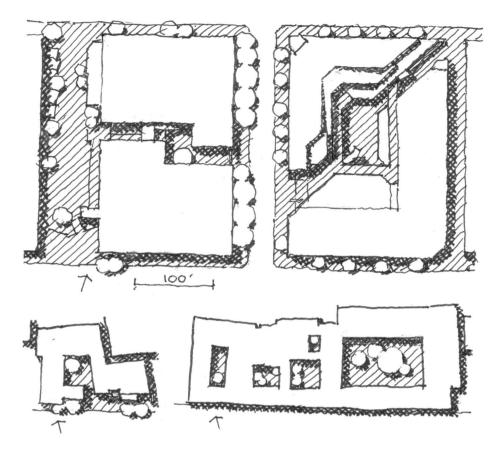

4.25 Ground plans of more fully defined central spaces. Above: The Cannery and Anchorage Square, San Francisco, CA. Below: Georgia O'Keefe Museum and Commercial Strip, Santa Fe, NM.

4.26 The Cannery, San Francisco: View to east in an entry passage. A dogleg stops the view at the small central courtyard, the vista also framed by bridges and stairs. Photo by 123RF.

of varying sizes. Being totally isolated from the street, these don't quite exemplify public urban spaces, but they do represent an ultimate version of "defined centers." These fully defined squares are, by design, somewhat sequestered from the life of the street: urban spaces with at least one exposure, such as the "alcove" cases, achieve both significant spatial containment and some degree of connection to urban life generally.

A few special cases round out these versions of defined centers (Fig. 4.27). San Diego's Horton Plaza, now extensively renovated, elaborated its deep midblock shopping "ravines" with bridges and towers. Completely inner-directed, it was criticized for turning its back on the outer streetwalls of its block, a balancing act that all such cases must address one way or another. At the other extreme in scale, Reno, Nevada's riverside "Eddy" music venue and bar defines and contains its patios with shipping containers that

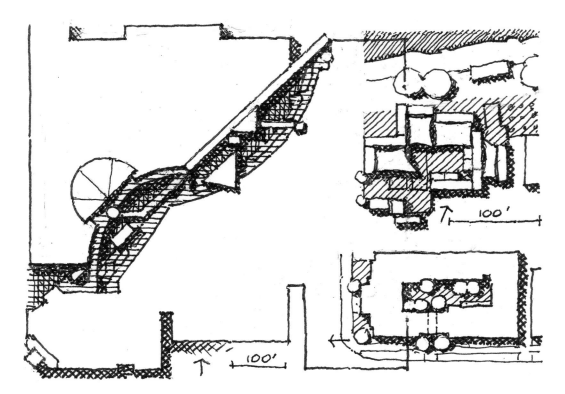

4.27 Ground plans of some unusual defined central spaces.
Clockwise (note differing scales): Horton Plaza, San Diego; "The Eddy," Reno; Rosewood Apartments, San Francisco.

house services, the open spaces partially sheltered by canvas canopies. And West Hollywood's Rosewood apartments exemplifies the residential archetype of the courtyard building, its tunnel-like entrance leading to a completely defined and sequestered garden court within.

• • •

Such fully defined spaces, even where a through-passing route is present, can't help but partake of a somewhat exclusive vibe in many cases. This comes down to the fact that they are likely to be embedded within a single project or development, as opposed to the multifarious nature of the settings of the campi, despite the latter's high degree of spatial definition. While one goal here has been to seek out ways urban spaces in America can best avoid being surrounded by streets and their cars, the fact remains that American city streets and sidewalks will continue to be car-intensive, and that those sidewalks will need a direct physical and visual link to an urban square if it is to be a vibrant public place. All of which is to say that "fully defined" spaces may sometimes be too isolated, and that "alcove" spaces like Spring Plaza, or well-defined "short linear" spaces like Rockville Town Square, may embody the best combination of demarcation from an American streetscape and connection to it.

5 Other Notes on America's Urban Spaces

Special Types

Civic buildings, as with county courthouses, are often sited in the center of a block, resulting in peripheral remnants of open space. While these spaces are sometimes handsomely landscaped, they can end up being window dressing and not especially notable as lively urban places. Churches also tend to have peripheral green spaces, and they sometimes also feature alcoves and cloisters, affording interesting urban form and space alike and thereby helping out some of the bleaker small towns. Since this effort focuses on the predominantly commercial and civic nature of downtown areas, findings in college and university campuses are typically not included here. But it bears noting that the spatial types and sequences (or not) on such campuses in the USA would provide material for another whole study.

Some of the campi feature peripheral through-passing canals which contribute their own family of unique and interesting features. The modern squares do sometimes incorporate water features, a desirable enhancement, though in such cases a careful weighing of the demands of their continuing maintenance is merited. Actual canals as features of modern urban open space, flanked by walks and amenities, appear in San Antonio and Oklahoma City among other cities. Threading their way through picturesque sequences, they bear witness to their value as foci of urban activity where conditions permit. In contrast, extensive residential canal systems, such as at Fort Lauderdale and Cape Coral, Florida, usually fail to incorporate such urban activity.

Urban spaces representative of all the "types" can be found adjoining rivers that have been revived as attractors for urban life, as in Providence, Reno, Little Rock, Chicago, Chattanooga, and many other cities and towns. Such spaces have a precedent of sorts in Campi de la Carita and San Vidal, as well as the Piazzetta.

Special Features

Most American city and town centers are orthogonal grids, typically relieved only by unavoidable interruptions such as rivers, railroads, and the demands of topography. As a result, the acute- and obtuse-angled boundaries that contribute to the more "organic" qualities of many of the campi are seldom in evidence. It's the older cities and towns of New England that present some welcome irregularities in their street networks, and a notable resource of intriguingly irregular and non-orthogonal urban form and space, as in Boston; Concord, New Hampshire; or Portland, Maine.

Some modern-day urban spaces accord more importance to intricate paving patterns than they really merit, their qualities often being only vaguely discernible from eye level. Sometimes this pattern-making takes the place of a more significant incorporation of amenity elements.

The level topography of Venice and the campi is regarded as an advantage in this study, the special nature of sloped or stepped spaces being a complication in the effort to check out findings among the likewise often flat urban spaces of modern America. Significant exceptions do appear, though, where site topography has resulted in level changes, monumental steps, and the like, adding dimensional variety, or at level changes that were introduced artificially for their presumed desirable qualities. A caveat applies when such level changes set an urban space apart in such a way that it contributes less effectively to the life of the street, as at the south exposure of El Paso's El Presidio Plaza or the west exposure of Cincinnati's Fountain Square.

The courthouse square with its peripheral lawn is included among these types for its ubiquity and its place in the sequence, while other landscape-focused urban open spaces are not: such quads, parks, greens, and gardens are of another faith and order from the sorts of largely hardscape spaces more closely related to the campi.

Typology of Spatial Shape and Adjacency

"Open spaces" and "solid blocks" form opposite poles on our circle of urban open-space types, the other types being arrayed sequentially between them. All these are to be found among the typologies illustrated on the following page, being an exercise to uncover all the configurational possibilities within a nine-square block (Fig. 5.1). Thinking of these as city blocks, they reveal many further ways to configure one, two, or more contiguous or adjoining urban spaces. (It bears noting that "mirrored" versions are not considered different, and that each is the same version regardless of rotation.) It should also be noted that some spatial configurations in our example projects that were regarded as undesirably open and ill-defined find their places in the array as well. One could consider the open space option (A1) as an abstract version of Pioneer Courthouse Square, with understood aspects of surrounding streets and urban sidewalls beyond. Further options, such as omitting one or more peripheral streets or adding one or more options on the sides, are necessarily beyond this scope. Notable among these versions are possibilities that take the following into account:

- Various applications of smaller freestanding elements as partial definers.
- Diagonal spatial adjacencies (regarding "touching corner" conditions as potential spatial links).
- Multiple separate smaller spaces as an alternative to large, single spaces.

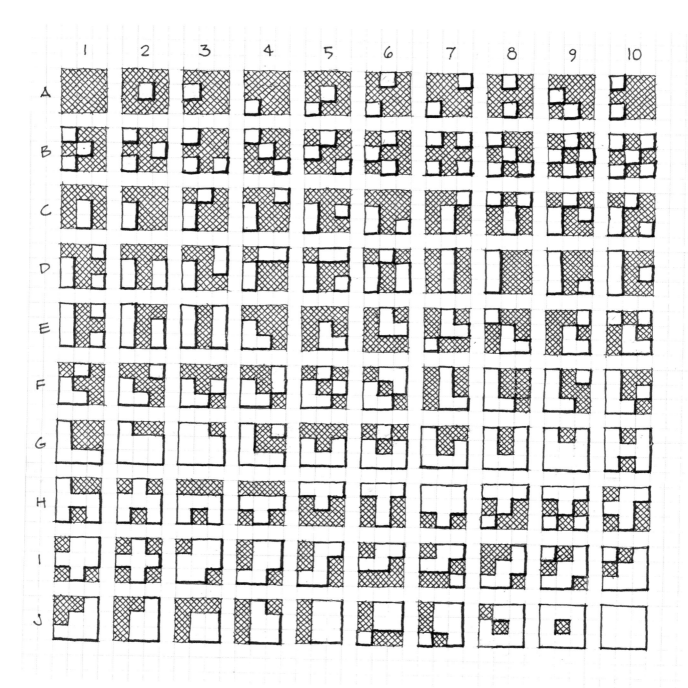

5.1 Typology of spatial shape and adjacency.

- Interestingly shaped spaces that turn corners, or are based on "H," "J," "T," "U," "Y," or "Z" configurations.
- Bounding an open space with corner elements to increase its interest and delay its reveal on approach.
- Various means to "wall off" one or more bounding streets.

These could be considered somewhat abstract diagrams of ways to either adapt existing conditions of urban space or to plan new ones. It takes some imagination to visualize how these can work with changes in proportion or with non-orthogonal shapes and boundaries, but the array serves as a resource of possibilities that might otherwise have gone undiscovered.

6 Conclusions

This unscientific sampling of urban open spaces in the USA has revealed that one or another of the "findings" about the campi are manifest in many modern counterparts. In each case they serve as examples, along with the campi themselves, of good practices in existing squares, of ways to improve existing squares, and of ways to influence the design of new ones. But in addition to the somewhat random ways in which they've done the right thing, these spaces inevitably have shortcomings. A review of the findings from the campi in light of these observations of modern squares is revealing:

Sequenced entry occurs quite seldom: modern squares are, more often than not, conceived as singular experiences rather than as parts of an ensemble. While isolated squares may have the benefit of impact and surprise, sequential experiences can be richer and more varied. In Venice it's often the campielli, when serving as foyers to campi beyond, that enhance the experience of both spaces through mutual contrast and surprise. The PSU Urban Center, Paley Park, and Patriots Park are among the modern squares benefiting from such entry spaces (Fig. 6.1).

An **obscured view in**, if taken to the levels often seen in the campi, may sometimes be considered problematic from a security standpoint for modern-day spaces. But the opposite case of a wide-open approach sacrifices the clear benefits of variety and surprise upon entry. As is often the case, a "happy medium" is called for, here one of partial exposure and partial delayed reveal. The zigzag configuration often seen at entries to the campi, as at San Stefano and San Zanipolo, affords a way to retain a broad entry path while also sheltering the bulk of a space from immediate view. Intervening elements at Larkin and Palmer Squares exemplify one such approach, while constrained entry routes, as at Mallory and Eagle Squares, are another way to delay the view in (Fig. 6.2).

Diagonal routes through work well in many of these cases, the courthouse squares excepted, though

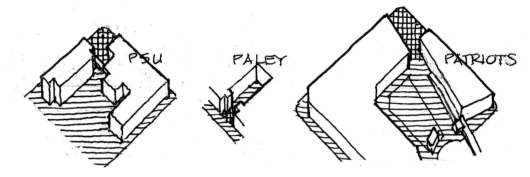

6.1 Cases of sequenced entry to urban spaces.

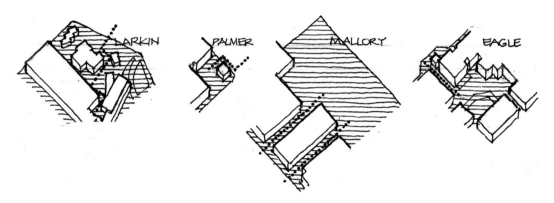

6.2 Cases of an obscured view in on approach.

some are configured to favor orthogonal crossings. A benefit of diagonal pedestrian routes, as opposed to an orthogonal, "one-point perspective" approach, is that angled relationships to buildings and other elements afford a more dynamic experience. Exemplars include Larkin Square, the PSU Urban Center, Eagle Square, and Anchorage Square (Fig. 6.3).

Activity, notably programmed activity, is in evidence in most cases. But some appear to provide a large, open space that is truly activated only when a correspondingly large group is gathered. A case may be made that there is often an unwarranted preference for very large urban plazas as signifiers of a successful downtown. These can end up being underpopulated much of the time, thus undercutting that very goal—Boston's City Hall Plaza being one well-known example. The intrusion of vehicular streets brings an "activity" of an undesirable sort, with obvious drawbacks of noise, pollution, general distraction, and an undoing of spatial definition. The range of spatial types demonstrates the successive benefits of one, two, or more "engaged" peripheries, resulting both in the removal of traffic and the adjacency of sidewall activity.

Elements of **amenity** comprise a short list of basic features in the campi, which don't require a lot of embellishment to be memorable. In the modern squares, elements of **furniture** come into play as well in what sometimes constitutes an overkill of furbishment, as in the case

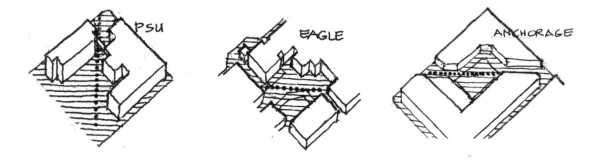

6.3 Cases of diagonal routes through urban spaces.

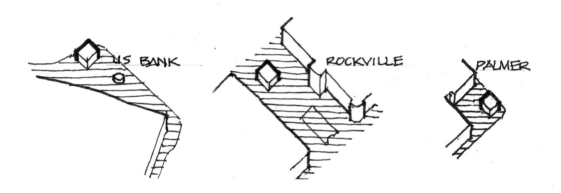

6.4 Cases of amenity in the form of freestanding kiosks.

of elaborate water features, rockwork, planters, pergolas, and the like. Striking a happy medium with such enhancements can seem an elusive goal. The role of the freestanding booth or kiosk, as at US Bank Plaza, Rockville Town Square, or Palmer Square, is clearly of significance as a surprisingly effective spatial definer and, to be sure, as a generator of activity when it houses vendors of food, drink, or information (Fig. 6.4).

Scale is concerned with sizing spaces appropriately to the activities they house. Again, many of the modern-day cases were found to be simply too big, overreaching a perceived goal of civic importance. While some of these large spaces do seem to be successfully attracting people to spend time in a variety of ways, there is an inevitable lack of a "sense of place" for individuals and small groups. Such a sense is palpably present in smaller, more intimately scaled urban spaces such as Palmer, Ghirardelli, Haymarket, Bicentennial, and Eagle Squares. The upshot: a range of scales in a city's urban spaces is called for, as opposed to a single large plaza, and smaller spaces that are more attuned to human scale need better representation in the modern urban world.

Sequence among these modern spaces, as a feature of the urban tour, is unusual: more typically, modern urban spaces are isolated in a matrix of solid blocks. That said, "linked spatial sequences" do achieve such an experience,

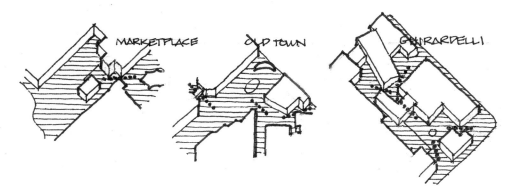

6.5 Cases of urban spaces engaged in a sequence.

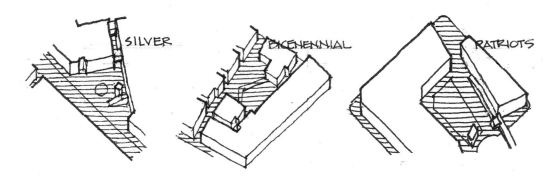

6.6 Cases of spatial variegation.

involving varied spatial types. A linked sequence involves multiple spaces connected at pinch points or links that set off their differing natures. Larkin Square, Market Place, Old Town Square, and Ghirardelli Square embody such linked sequences (Fig. 6.5). The typical urban experience of a streetscape grid would benefit from an ordered sprinkling of one or another of the open-space types, at a variety of scales, forming such a sequence. Examples in Venice—notably those centering on Campi Santa Margherita and San Stefano, and the link between San Stefano and San Marco—suggest the idea of repurposing amenable modern alleyways as pedestrian connectors, their intimate scale contrasting both with streets and the open spaces they connect.

Spatial Variegation, as manifest in the campi, includes projecting elements, engaged towers, and combinations of obtuse, acute, concave, and/or convex sidewall relationships. The modern squares, though, are often straitjacketed by their context of an orthogonal grid. As referenced regarding *amenity*, "open" or engaged spaces could be notably variegated by the addition of one or more outbuildings, especially if judicious angled relationships are employed. Modern such cases include Miller Plaza, Larkin Square, Veterans Plaza, Market Place, Silver Plaza, and Patriots Park. Irregular boundaries are also inherently likely to result in more

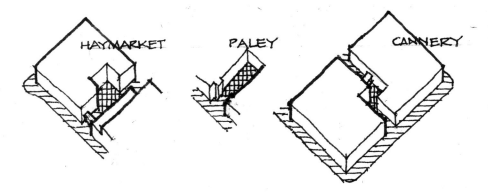

6.7 Cases of proportion that approach the comfortable limits of height vs size.

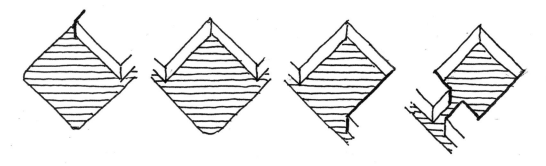

6.8 Cases of increasing degrees of spatial definition.

interesting spaces, as in the examples at Portland, Maine, and Concord, New Hampshire (Fig. 6.6).

Sidewall Variegation in the modern squares is, on the face of it, quite a different animal than in the campi, for not only are there often significant gaps between buildings, but they can vary considerably in height. Many modern cases do, however, exhibit the wide variety of opening size, type, and placement, as well as the "fractal scalability," for which the campi are notable. In the unusual case of Piazza San Marco, not only are its repetitive and consistent sidewalls full of detail incident, but they incorporate a suite of exceptional and varied "foreground" elements. Modern-day situations where an effort has been made to render the sidewalls repetitive and consistent can fail to convincingly emulate those distinctive qualities, doing the contained spaces no favors.

Opinions differ about **proportion** when it comes to urban squares. Some rules of thumb for agreeable ratios are noted in the findings. For another, Sitte opined that "the height of its principal building, taken once, can be declared to be roughly the minimum dimension for a plaza; the absolute maximum that still gives a good effect being the double of that height. . ."[22] Surprisingly, experience offers that when high-rise buildings adjoin modern squares, they don't necessarily overwhelm them, perhaps because anything above three or four stories is beyond one's normal cone of vision (excepting, of course, when looking upward). That said, tall sidewalls encroaching on all sides, particularly if the space is modest in size, will make it seem more of a light well than a space for people. (And, ironically, one of the main problems of a light well is the way it cuts off natural light.) Although they approach this limit, the small courts of Haymarket Square, Paley Park, and the Cannery are successful in the service of both definition and intrigue (Fig. 6.7). In the special case of pedestrianized streets, although they differ from squares by virtue of their length, they can still constitute interesting urban places, even though inevitably imbued with a sense of "linear movement" and, typically, a lack of spatial variegation.

Lastly, among the campi **spatial definition** ranges from fully defined spaces to "alcove" situations facing significant water elements. By contrast, modern squares often adjoin through-passing streets on all sides, resulting in a notable lessening of room-like character. In another frequent aspect of spatial definition among the Venetian squares, protruding elements conceal part of the space from view. This aspect of "intrigue" is far less common among the modern squares—cropping up primarily among linked spatial sequences and defined centers when it does occur—with fully revealed quadrilateral spaces being more the general rule. The "alcove" as a modern-day spatial type deserves more widespread representation (Fig. 6.8).

• • •

If there is any single generalization to be made on the basis both of the Venetian campi and the modern American squares, it's a need for paying attention to what an urban space is or should be *for*. Grand plazas are well and good, but they call for complementary outdoor living spaces characterized by human scale, definition, variegation, and intrigue. And while the campi evolved over long periods of time, the modern squares typically took form intentionally, as planned initiatives. The degree to which they bring focus to the life of the city, while also achieving their own sense of place—and transcending, in a sense, their "designed" origins—makes them suitable partners for the campi in typifying these lessons for successful urban spaces.

Endnotes

1. A few examples from new towns or developments, selected from many: Camden, South Carolina's town square is surrounded by perpendicular parking. Seaside, Florida's central square was surrounded by perpendicular parking until 2020; it remains to be seen whether it will be restored in the future. Nearby Rosemary Beach's town greens—actually wide medians—are flanked by angled parking. These cases recall the precedent of American courthouses squares, which have streets and parking on all sides.

2. This fact, while true for pedestrian circulation in Venice, must admit the occasionally compromising aspect of vehicular circulation on the canals, in the form of a variety of motorized craft.

3. The campi have been called the epitome of good urban spaces. (Lennard, Suzanne H. Crowhurst, and Henry L. Lennard. *Livable Cities*. Southampton, NY: Gondolier Press. 1987: 133. This resource includes a good description of the general nature of the campi and how they are used, rendering it a useful complement to this discussion.)

4. Convention varies as to the italicization of foreign names and terms. For the sake of simplicity such terms are not here italicized.

5. These squares were selected primarily for their evident success as vibrant urban places, along with a few that demonstrate cautionary issues. Many other campi are of interest, but to feature a larger number would have been unproductively repetitive. The selection was intended to cover a range of scale, character, and activity in hopes that useful commonalities across this range would appear.

6. Alexander saw fit to use a snapshot of this campo as the frontispiece to the section on small public squares in *A Pattern Language*. (Alexander, Christopher, Sara Ishikawa, and Murray Silverstein. *A Pattern Language*. Berkeley, CA: Oxford University Press, 1977: 310.)

7. Sottoporteghi are low, tunnel-like exterior passageways linking campi, streets, and/or canals. While likely to be considered security risks in a modern context, they afford some striking sequential contrasts in the Venetian urban tour.

8. Evidently attractive to filmmakers, this campo has seen Katharine Hepburn fall in the canal in *Summertime*, and Harrison Ford and company clamber out of a simulated manhole in *Indiana Jones and the Last Crusade*.

9. Until recent times one of but three pedestrian bridges over the Grand Canal, the heavy timber framed Accademia and the others have been joined by a controversial Calatrava-designed bridge near the train station. Hundreds of more modest stepped canal bridges represent a ubiquitous and characteristic exception to the "no topography" aspect of Venice.

10. Honour, Hugh. *Fodor's Venice*. New York, NY: David McKay Company, Inc., 1971: 190.

11. On the website www.newurbanism.org, among a familiar list of ten principles of New Urbanism, that of "connectivity" has been fittingly illustrated by a figure-ground plan of Campi San Stefano, Sant'Angelo and environs.

12. Jan Gehl notes: "A walking network with alternating street spaces and small squares often will have the psychological effect of making the walking distances seem shorter. The trip is subdivided naturally, in manageable stages." (Gehl, Jan. *Life Between Buildings*. Washington, D.C.: Island Press, 2011: 141.)

13. In *The Stones of Venice,* Volume 3.

14. For a detailed study of this campo: Carrera, Fabio. *Campo Santa Maria Formosa, Venice, Italy: A case study of the application of visual, dynamic and scale-invariant analysis for the description, interpretation and evaluation of City Form.* 11.330 Theory of City Form Final Paper, Massachusetts Institute of Technology, Cambridge, MA, 1997.

15. Santa Maria dei Miracoli is unique among the churches of Venice in being completely freestanding. (Honour 1917: 331.)

16. Alexander asserts the only exceptions they know of to be the likes of Piazza San Marco and Trafalgar Square, which are in "great town centers teeming with people." (Alexander, Ishikawa, and Silverstein 1977: 311.)

17. Lynch, Kevin. 1962. *Site Planning.* Cambridge, MA: MIT Press, as quoted in Gehl 2011, 163.

18. Thadani, Dhiru A. *Visions of Seaside.* New York, NY: Rizzoli, 2013: 409.

19. The courthouse square plan types are based on Dr. Marian Moffett's study of county seats in Tennessee.

20. The procedure for finding the various types and locations of urban spaces in the USA that are the basis for this section took full advantage of the online resources of Google Maps. The states were called up in sequence, the central areas of the cities and larger towns were tracked across from above, and apparent cases of one or another type of urban open space were zoomed into and examined, as well as looked at from "street view" vantage points. Browser searches for urban open spaces were also made, though these generally tended to find large parks and plazas rather than the smaller "anomalies" that were often of more interest. While angled or perpendicular parking was unusual on the peripheries of the squares selected for study, parallel parking was quite common, and street frontages on two, three, or four sides were very much the rule.

21. A significant number of pedestrianized streets exist, including at Boulder, Colorado; St. Augustine, Florida; Miami Beach, Florida; Boston, Massachusetts; Helena, Montana; Schenectady, New York; Burlington, Vermont; Charlottesville, Virginia; and Cape May, New Jersey. The "mallification" of streets, a trend dating to the 1970s, has not always been successful, many such efforts having not stood the test of time.

22. Collins, George R., and Christiane Crasemann Collins. Camillo Sitte: *The Birth of Modern City Planning.* New York, NY: Rizzoli, 1986: 182.

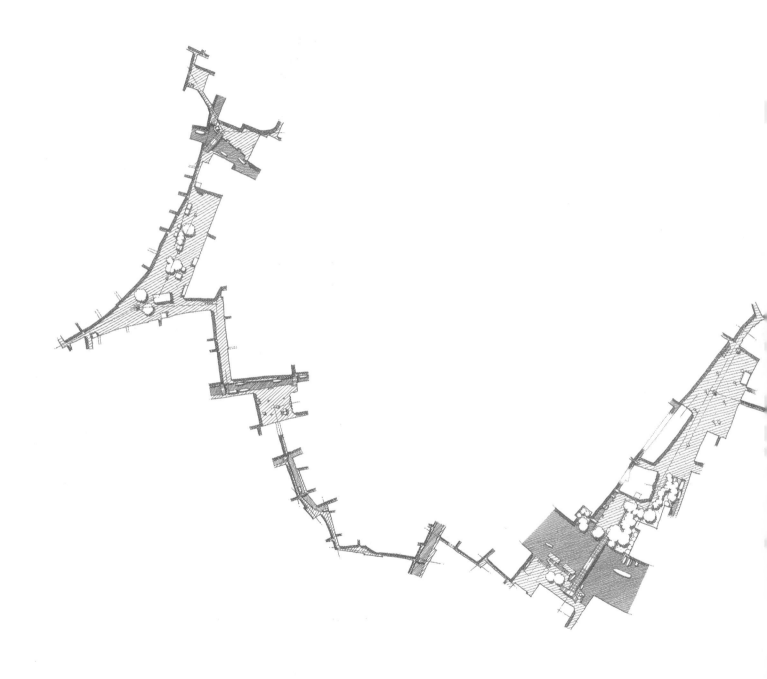

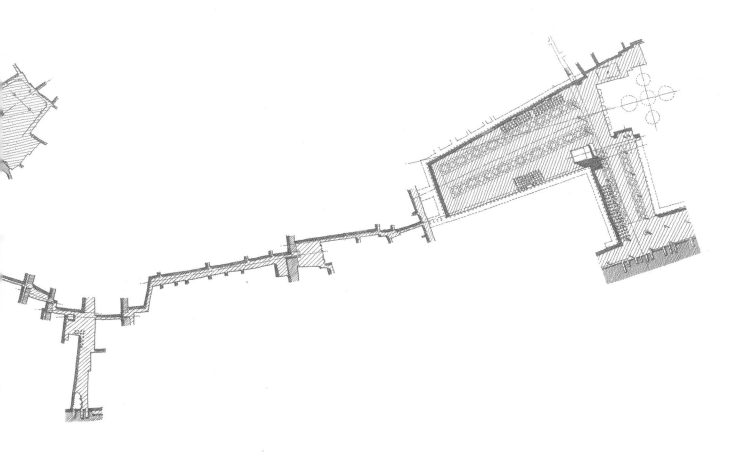